BUDDING TEENS

Understanding Adolescence

BUDDING TEENS
Understanding Adolescence

Sushila Singhal
Pratibha Dua

ATLANTIC
PUBLISHERS & DISTRIBUTORS (P) LTD

Published by

ATLANTIC

PUBLISHERS & DISTRIBUTORS (P) LTD

7/22, Ansari Road, Darya Ganj,
New Delhi-110002
Phones : +91-11-40775252, 23273880, 23275880, 23280451
Fax : +91-11-23285873
Web : www.atlanticbooks.com
E-mail : orders@atlanticbooks.com

Branch Office
5, Nallathambi Street, Wallajah Road,
Chennai-600002
Phones : +91-44-64611085, 32413319
E-mail : chennai@atlanticbooks.com

ISBN 978-81-269-1340-4

Printed in India at Glorious Printers, A-13, DSIDC, Jhilmil Industrial Area, Delhi-110095

Dedicated to

Millions of adolescents braving their growing years

Acknowledgements

While we acknowledge the special support of our families in multiple ways, we are indebted to many for help in this endeavour. We are thankful to Dr. U.N.B. Rao, Chairman of the Urivi Vikram Charitable Trust for persistently pushing us to complete the book; Prof. Daya Pant of NCERT and Dr. Jaswant Kaur of George Brown College, Toronto, Canada for reading parts of the book and commenting on them; adolescents' mothers—Namita Sahgal and Renu Shukla for reading chapters and making constructive suggestions; young adults—Shruti, Rishab and their friends for commenting on the relevance of various issues of adolescent behaviour in the light of their own growing-up experiences; and loving adolescents—Neha, Viraj, Mira and Shivani for talking about the diverse problems and the perspectives they experienced.

Sushila Singhal
Pratibha Dua

Preface

Adolescents are the backbone of a country. They constitute nearly 22% of the population in India and are important trend-setters in the society. Their interests are at the centre of planning—economic, socio-cultural, health care, education and the democratic polity. They are powerful consumers promoting the economy, agents of socio-cultural changes, mainstay of educational systems, and important pillars of democracy. Their voices are important in all domains. They embody a tremendous amount of untapped positive energy and resourcefulness that gets released and set in motion in the process of growing up supported by adults, central to action. Adolescents' strengths and orientations need to be fully comprehended, and reinforced in all spheres of activity and programmes of education, training, counseling and research, among others, adopting a proactive approach.

The book *Budding Teens* is published in support of the authors' personal concerns and interests and of Urivi Vikram Charitable Trust, New Delhi in the growth and well-being of adolescents. It signals the continued interest and concern of the authors and the trust in this direction. Prior to this publication, two books had been published for the trust, *Teenage Blues* authored by Vimala Veeraraghavan and Shalini Singh (1999) and *Adolescent Concerns Through Their Own Eyes* by Sushila Singhal and U.N.B. Rao (2004). Both of these publications reckoned that adolescence was a distinct stage of life needing attention of planners, policymakers, educationists, medical specialists and parents. The analyses made to write those books yielded very meaningful results to indicate that a good per cent of adolescents across different age groups were strongly concerned about financial, academic, psychological, health, family and social issues that affect their lives. The gaps between the perceived needs and the realization pointed to the areas of necessary interventions for adolescents, parents and teachers. But, there existed an intensified need for addressing the concerns expressed earlier and the emerging powerful challenges the adolescents, parents and teachers face day in and day out. The challenges necessitated the adoption of a humane and professional approach in order to promote a better understanding among adolescents, parents, teachers and counselors—the main pressure point that triggered the writing of this book.

The book has evolved from our deep concern to provide to the parents, teachers, other adults and the adolescents the experience of a joyful ride through rough and tough, pleasure and pain inherent in the process of growing up. Adults have commonly reported difficulties in dealing with adolescents, and in recognizing the lows and highs adolescents have to go through. Adolescents today are globally connected and live in a futuristic society. They are exposed to the compatible culture shocks of trends in music, fashions, technology, etc. They are under tremendous pressure to be prepared for the technologically complex jobs, and a continuous upgrading of their skills and even periodic changes in jobs. This suggests that while the genetic-psychological factors still display the same pattern of development, the environmental conditions of growing up, the contents, methodology of learning and social networking are becoming incrementally complex. Obviously, adolescents are under pressure and yet are able to adhere to changes faster than adults, while adults (parents, teachers and counselors, etc.) have greater difficulty in adjusting to the new socio-cultural and technological context, and in understanding and appreciating the changed attitudes and behaviour of adolescents.

The book has tried to move away from the conventional approach, which looked at adolescence as a stormy phase of life. It adopts a developmental perspective and views adolescents as active participants in their development in multiple domains, in interaction with parents, teachers and other adults. The onus is on parents and teachers to redefine their roles from controlling to identifying, and reinforcing the strengths of adolescents in a spirit of joy, love and acceptance and enjoy the experience of moving along with adolescents. The emphasis is on positive perception, encouragement, communication, nurturance, and guidance to enable the adolescents to enjoy their growing years, feel comfortable, and stay positive about their present and future. The adolescents need acceptance, support and guidance of parents, teachers and others to realize the positive benefits of their potential growth, not curbs that threaten to distort their development, alienate, and inculcate negativism and cynicism in them. Parents, teachers and others should relate, communicate and guide them in identifying their resources, skills, and personal predispositions and develop them constructively to become loving and empowered young adults.

The book should be considered a positive help suggesting some useful steps to follow and strategies to adopt. No book can or should claim to offer solutions to all problems even in one domain. This one does not either. Each adolescent is a different human being having different capabilities, resources, and facilities at his/her disposal and faces different kinds of challenges. Each one tends to grow differently, have different experiences and problems, and is able to achieve solutions differently. The book proposes to be useful to a large audience of parents, teachers, counselors, educational administrators and adolescents themselves. It has tried to include most of the prominent issues touching the lives of adolescents. Some of the issues are quite sensitive and complex, yet the attempt has been made to present them in a very lucid, concise and complete form using simple language and cases as illustrations.

The book comprises a total of 12 chapters. Each chapter focuses on a distinct issue and yet stays very much connected to others as an adolescent is one whole unit. Each chapter includes some conceptualization of the issue, discussion of some relevant cases and analyses, how those are to be dealt with in the system, and what parents, teachers and others can do to help adolescents pursue their growth leads. It is hoped that parents, teachers and counselors would find this book useful.

Sushila Singhal
Pratibha Dua

Contents

1

Assets and Challenges of Adolescence

Life is tough, and if you have the ability to laugh at it you have the ability to enjoy it.

Salma Hayek

Veena, Kavita and Anjali are close friends. So are Vipin, Hem and Rohan. They talk about their growing up as a passage from childhood into adulthood. They often lament 'we do not remember of any stage in our lives experienced as adolescence. Once we were past 10 or 11 years we were expected to share some work with adults in the family, girls with mothers and aunts and boys with fathers, uncles, cousins etc. and these were particularly the physically hard tasks, such as cleaning the house for girls, and carrying heavy things for boys. We had little to engage in terms of hobbies or extra-curricular activities. You considered yourself lucky if you got to the college. We had little to get entertained, dress up and go out. Now how different it has become for our kids. They have assured education, opportunities of dressing up, outings and entertainment. In fact, all that they need is assured to most of them, yet they are constantly asking for more. It gives us tremendous pleasure to see them growing up, enjoying their freedom, and developing variety of skills.' This makes one to reckon the abundant positives that should be unfolding during adolescence.

Unfolding Agenda

Adolescence, since Hall wrote about it, has been accepted as a distinct stage of human development located between childhood and adulthood, when the child is neither very young nor very old. It is more than a merger of childhood into adulthood. The age range accepted by World Health Organization (WHO) is between 10-19 years. This period is marked by changes in the person on all developmental dimensions (physical, cognitive, affective and behavioural), heightened social expectations, new roles, and uncertainties. The developing adolescent undergoes rapid physical changes accompanied by simultaneous cognitive, emotional and behavioural changes. It is a phase marked by evolving sexuality. Alongwith the growing body, adolescents develop more systematic thinking. They become capable of abstract thinking and of conceptualizing, reasoning and understanding with logic. They tend to become idealistic and interested in deriving own theories. They like to make their own decisions. They have tools of intensified language ability and can learn multiple languages. They have high emotional sensitivity and the attraction towards opposite sex is on the rise as a natural corollary of growth. They develop the capacity to love and being loved. They question everything, become more independent and/or strive incrementally towards it. They become distant from parents, and close in relationships with friends. The intimacy with peer group increases as it becomes important to them to create new opportunities to interact with the outside world and explore it without adult surveillance/restrictions. They enjoy being part of the peer group. Adolescents experience sudden mood swings from feeling extremely happy to extremely sad. They become temperamental and are often not understood and appreciated by adults around. They like to take interest in trying out new products, styles, roles and everything that can catch the eye. They show marked sensitivity and high fantasy. They are in search of an answer to 'Who am I'? Overall, it is a phase of highs and lows characterized by multiple creative dreams and confusions about one's physical, intellectual, emotional and social self, and career.

The multidimensional development during adolescence enables children in unfolding their developmental assets and presents a number of challenges to them and their socializing agents (parents, teachers and significant others). It is observed that the assets and challenges the 10-11 years old face are different than the 18 years old. The period is thus divided into three phases—early, middle and late adolescence. During each phase new assets unfold and pose new challenges with some overlaps and more differences. Some of the assets and challenges implicit in different developmental domains are discussed in the following pages:

Physical Domain

Assets. The development of assets in the physical domain during adolescence encompass many of the dramatic changes and growth in body size, improved gross and fine motor skills, and biological maturity. Until the age of 8-9 years, the child grows physically at a slower rate, but thereafter the rate of growth becomes accelerated. Now an endocrine gland called the pituitary gland, situated at the base of the brain, becomes active. From its lofty position, it sends signals to the thyroid gland, adrenal glands, ovaries and testes, directing them to produce the thyroid hormones, cortisol, estrogen, testosterone respectively. These hormones have dramatic effects on metabolism, blood pressure, reproduction, and other vital body functions.

At around 9 years of age, most children begin to display signs of accelerated growth, but it takes place at different rates for girls and boys. The growth spurts are experienced by children for a brief period of 2-3 years, occurring nearly two years earlier in girls than boys. In girls the growth spurt is visible between 10-13 years whereas in boys it may occur between 11-16 years, nearly reaching the peak around 12 years in girls and 14 years in boys. There is significant gain in height, size of internal organs as well as changes in skeletal and muscular systems. The bones grow faster than muscles and some adolescents encounter coordination challenges, like the failure of muscles and tendons to adequately protect the bones. There are individual differences in development among girls as well as boys depending upon the heredity, the region from which one comes and the climate. The changes that take place in the reproductive system are of two types, namely, the internal changes in the primary sex characteristics (genitalia), and the associated or external changes called the secondary sex characteristics (e.g., breast development in girls; facial hair in boys). The external changes make the boys and girls look different from each other. The process of rapid physical changes in adolescents signals the onset of puberty. It sets in motion a cascade of hormones that facilitate the development of primary and secondary sex characteristics. Girls start these changes before boys (10 vs 12 years or so) and appear to be maturing much faster for the first three or four years. After this boys catch up.

The puberty sets in girls 2-3 years earlier than boys. It is marked in females by the onset of menstruation, and in males by the occurrence of nocturnal emissions (wet dreams) because of the build-up of seminal fluid. For most children puberty is a time of discovery. The increased production of adrenal hormones affects skeletal growth, hair production and skin changes. These highly visible changes and different rates of maturity make many adolescents feel uncomfortable with their changing body. The speed of physical changes may induce in some adolescents a higher concern about their appearance.

Besides the physical changes, with the onset of puberty certain changes occur in the thinking process, emotional state and in the socialization patterns of adolescents. The fluctuations in their basal metabolism cause periods of restlessness and lassitude. They tend to 'have ravenous appetites and peculiar tastes' and have a propensity for improper nutrition. The focus in the choice of foods shifts to what tastes good from what is healthy and nutritious. Some of them develop poor physique and become vulnerable to illness and bad health. The physical growth and development uses a lot of energy because of which teenagers need more sleep and they do have deep and longer sleep.

Challenges. The onset of puberty presents a major challenge for the adolescent as well as parents, associated with physical growth and changes in body. It is now taking place in all countries earlier than in the past or what it used to be in their parents' time. In some cases it starts even before the age of 10 years. The puberty induces in the child as well as parents a lot of confusions, apprehensions and anxiety. The child needs time to understand what is happening to his/her body. Child feels confused as s/he is neither a child nor a grown up. So do the adults, often wondering about their child looking suddenly big and different. 'How do we help the child in dealing with what s/he is going through?' It is reported to be a much more difficult contingency experienced by females and their parents than males. The adolescents are curious about their evolving sexuality, what is happening to them and why? How should they deal with it as the social norms do not permit them to talk about it openly? They look at their own body and of others, and do not understand why at the same age they are growing differently? Is there something wrong with them and if so, how to talk about it? How should they handle their growing body as every time their size changes they even feel that they look odd? Where and how to get the needed information and how to get the help from parents and others on such issues that have been treated as social taboos so far?

Cognitive Domain

Assets. In this domain the focus is on intellectual development, which refers to the increased ability of adolescents to understand the situations and the issues, and to reason out the how and why of them with some logic. In early adolescents, intellectual development is not noticed as clearly as the physical development, but certainly it is as intense. Many of the early adolescents exhibit wide variations in the range of individual intellectual development, meta-cognition (the ability to think about one's own thinking), and independent thinking. They are highly curious and display a broad array of interests though not many of these interests are sustained in later years. Typically, most adolescents are eager to learn about topics and areas they find interesting and useful for them, favour active over passive learning experiences, and prefer to interact with peers during educational and other activities.

Adolescence marks the onset of complex thinking that includes in-depth questioning. Adolescents between 12 to 18 years are at the "formal operations" stage of Piaget. It is characterized by an increased independence of thinking through problems and situations. They are expected to develop an understanding of pure abstractions, such as philosophy and higher math concepts. They should be able to learn and apply general information needed to adapt to specific situations, and learn occupation specific information and skills. A major component of the passage through adolescence is the achievement of cognitive transition as adolescents can think in more advanced, efficient and more complex ways than children.

Most adolescents succeed in acquiring the capacity for abstract thought processes by late adolescence, but the transition to higher levels of cognitive functioning differs significantly across individuals as well as across and within content areas. They show an improved ability to think about the future, anticipate needs, and develop personal goals in more than one ways. For example, now their thinking tends to move beyond what they already believe, know and understand. They are able to imagine hypothetical situations and think of solutions. They can comprehend the higher-order, abstract logic inherent in puns, proverbs, metaphors, and analogies. They can apply their advanced reasoning and logical processes to think and articulate different social and ideological issues, argue from an adopted stance/position, and appreciate the subtle and sophisticated levels of humour in text/discussions. They think about the process of thinking itself, and display increased ability to introspect and be self-conscious. Their thinking becomes multidimensional, rather than limited to a single issue. They have also been able to do away with their belief in absolutism. Positions and things are seen now in a relative perspective. They are more likely to question others' assertions and less likely to accept facts as absolute truths.

Difficulties arise often in relationships, when adolescents begin seeing the values and positions of adults around (parents, teachers) as relativistic and needing change. Their higher capacity for analytical thought, reflection and introspection also signifies that they have developed morally at the same time. Late adolescents acquire the capacity to reconcile their understanding of adults around them with their own views. They accomplish successfully the transition from a self-centered perspective to having consideration for the rights and feelings of others. Even when they are aware of weaknesses and flaws in the views and positions taken by others, they are reticent to accept their own flaws.

During adolescence children go through middle, secondary and senior secondary schooling. The studies become important. Every day a major part of their waking hours are spent in school. The school environment is important as it gives or constrains the opportunities for increased interactions with peers and teachers. In a positive school environment, there are many more opportunities to explore and learn that can affect the adolescents on a long-term basis and the vice versa. Adolescents acquire new ways of behaving and conducting themselves. New values are learnt and the values acquired at home are assigned new meanings. The schools alongwith providing the variety of exposures set certain limits and standards of achievement in different curricular and co-curricular domains. They are required to participate in different activities. They need to excel in as many areas as possible and those who cannot reach the competitive standards try to find alternate means to seek recognition. These means may not always be in line with the spirit of setting the standards in the school. This produces lot of pressure on adolescents.

Challenges. Adolescents are under pressure to meet the academic expectations of teachers, parents and self in the cognitive domain. Individual teachers exercise pressure on them for good achievement in their subject. The teachers recognize individual differences and set different expectations for different students. The adolescents interact differently with teachers. Their individual ways of interacting make them responsive or avoiding type depending upon the nature and personality of the teacher. During this period studies are of major concern to students and parents. Each student has to cope with the academic work set for a particular level. If a student is able to reach the set level it gives her/him lot of encouragement and satisfaction, and one gets positive reinforcement from the adults in her/his context. Also there is competitiveness amongst classmates and peers of same age group. A higher achievement is valued in the society, which puts pressure on students. One is constantly exposed to class tests, term exams and Board exams. One is always expected to score higher than others and also one's earlier score and thus it becomes stressful.

In late adolescence, they have the challenge of opting for a future career. Some students are clear about their career line by this time, but most are confused as to what stream/line they would choose and how they will settle in their career. Parental expectations and their preset standards for students add to their confusion. The challenges for adolescents are of coping with the demand to regularly attend the school, the pressure of studies and examinations, to prepare for separation from parents, find a career, become perfectionist, learn to remain cool and resilient and do well also in adverse circumstances.

Affective Domain

Assets. The source of emotional development lies into the interactions of the adolescents with people (parents, peers and other significant persons) and situations in their context. It is believed that a good intellectual development ensures the ability of good analysis and understanding the reality and thus facilitates good emotional development. There is however, no one to one correspondence between intellectual and emotional development.

Adolescence is seen in general as a highly volatile and turbulent phase of life leaving most adolescents vulnerable to some emotional difficulties or the other. Early and middle adolescents are found busy in their constant search and effort to achieve independence and identity. It is the time of their life when they are seeking their own sense of individuality and uniqueness. They are searching for adult recognition and acceptance, what they want to be as adults, while striving to have the peer approval. As the base of social affiliation expands to include with family the peers, they begin to experience feelings of conflict due to the difficulty of competing allegiances from the two sources. They become more attuned to the differences between self and others, which complicates the task of achieving identity and self-discovery. The early adolescents, in general, feel things more intensely and are unpredictable. They are moody, restless, and even show erratic and inconsistent behaviour including anxiety, bravado, and fluctuations between superiority and inferiority. They are quite self-conscious, may have low self-esteem, and may not be able to take the criticism of their perceived personal shortcomings from others, inclusive of peers. Small things make them emotionally charged to put them at the threshold of resorting to childish behaviour, exaggeration of simple incidents, and one-sided arguments. They remain thus at risk in making decisions, which do not have in general positive consequences. They may continue to believe that their experiences, feelings, and problems are unique and uncommon. Many adolescents when emotionally troubled settle down easily, but some may resort to overeating, extra sleeping habit and an over-concern for appearance.

Challenges. As the adolescents try to assume adult roles marked changes are noticed in their behaviour that constitutes a formidable adjustment challenge to themselves and the adults around. There is high assertiveness, they want to make decisions for self and resent adult domination. They want freedom. There is high sense of morality and values. Any restriction leads to aggression. The age is marked by identity crisis. One is constantly trying to find out 'Who am I?' S/he is evolving and shaping personality around the perceptions of 'I.' All this gives rise to many issues. Adults in contact with adolescents i.e. mainly parents and teachers often wonder as to what is wrong with 'my' adolescent? They are often at loose ends about how to deal with them?

Parents often face a variety of dilemmas. 'Should I cut down his time with friends? Should I talk to his friend's parents? Should I ignore?' There is lot of discrepancy between adults' views of the adolescents and the adolescents themselves. Also the views are not congruent with the social norms. Parents complain that—'You have become very temperamental. You are showing your attitude. You have lost courtesy. Your moods are getting on our nerves.' Adolescents also complain that they are not understood by adults, are constantly criticized and undermined.

Parents often are not prepared to deal with the challenge that their adolescent is learning to hold her/his reins. Rather they suffer from the feeling that they have lost control or influence over their ward. Adolescents want parents to be clear and consistent about the rules and boundaries they set, but resent many of the restrictions on their growing freedom and ability to decide for them. The challenge for both is to learn to have patience and understanding of the mutual needs that can result in a pleasant dialogue. Experience suggests that adolescents are at greater risk of getting into trouble if their parents are not clear about what to tell them, and also if they do not know the whereabouts of their adolescent?

Social Domain

Assets. Social development refers to an adolescent's capacity for mature interactions with other individuals and groups. They develop close relationships outside the family, with peers and friends of their own age. Relationships within the family also change as they grow up. Real disagreements surface with the adolescents developing own views that are often not shared by their parents. Adolescents spend a lot of time with friends, or on the telephone/text message with each other. Despite this being an irritant to parents, it is an important way for the adolescents to move towards becoming more independent. The friendships are part of learning how to get along with other people and gaining a sense of identity different from the family. They like to dress up like peers, as clothes and appearance are a way of expressing solidarity with friends. The increase in closeness with peers increases the distance with parents. Parents often feel rejected but it is necessary for adolescents to develop their own identity. As they become more independent, they want to try out new things but often find that they have very little experience in making appropriate choices. This leads to uncertainty in their behaviour.

Adolescence is the time when people start to learn earnestly about the world they inhabit and to discover their place in it. This involves trying out different novel experiences, some of which may be risky or even dangerous. They may crave for doing exciting things, which is difficult for adults to understand and appreciate. Most manage to find their excitement in music, sports, or some other activities that involve a lot of energy expenditure and little physical risk. Some adolescents may experiment with drinks or drugs or smoking, and they do it usually in the company of friends. If anyone does this alone, they are in much greater danger. They accept warnings from older adolescents more readily than their parents.

Adolescents have a strong need to belong to a group, as peer approval becomes increasingly important with decrease in adult approval. As they mature socially, they experience opposing loyalties to peer group and family. The friendships, positive peer relationships and social interactions boost young adolescents' self-esteem. They try to learn group's lingo and behaviours. Many of them identify with their preferred peers, emulate them and make their own choices. They may however, continue to see family as a critical factor in final decision-making. They may be rebellious to parents and adults, but they still depend on them. They also try to test the limits of acceptable behaviour and engage in challenging adult authority. Feelings of adult rejection can drive adolescents into the somewhat secure social environment of their peer group. Social maturity comes rather slowly than physical and intellectual development. Consequently, there are times when adolescents over react to social situations, ridicule others and feel embarrassed. They are also socially vulnerable due to influences of media and negative interactions with adults. They take media as the last word in the absence of secure figures with whom to interact and discuss the contents of the received messages and learn what is right.

Adolescents encounter social expectations reminding them that now they look big and should behave in a socially desirable manner. The parental expectations are set for them depending upon their socio-economic origin, cultural and moral values, and upbringing. The conservative parents' expectations of the adolescent are different from those in the affluent group or intellectual parents. They are open to lot of exposure in the society. Changes are taking place in socio-cultural norms with societies becoming modern and loosening many of the constraints inbuilt in a traditional system. In the past what was considered a taboo has become a daily routine now. For example, the mixing up between girls and boys, more or less a taboo earlier, has become acceptable in the society. There is lot of emphasis among adolescents on partying, eating out and entertainment.

Challenges. Adolescents are constantly under pressure to find their place in the group and community. Adults in contact, mainly parents and teachers, often expect the adolescents to adapt rapidly according to the social situation. They expect them to behave like children in one context and like adults in another and thus add to their confusions. There is lot of discrepancy between adults' views of the adolescent and the adolescents themselves. Also they do not find it congruent with social norms. Parents keep on referring back to their time and compare their ward with their own childhood. They often complain—'When we were of your age, we did not do any such thing with friends. All the time you are partying. Close this loud music.' Adults more than often end up in preaching about social behaviour, whether by telling to do things their way or saying things sarcastically. The adults set standards that they resent and try to violate. The teens have own dreams, excitements and standards. They want to enjoy life. Friends are important for them. Being accepted and being part of the group is crucial.

Summing Up. The development in adolescence showed that numerous assets develop and challenges arise both for the adolescents and adult figures mainly from the changes occurring in the physical, cognitive, emotional and social domains. As the child progresses in age from year to year physically, academically, behaviourally and socially, most parents feel it to be a matter of pride. They also express their concerns and worries about how to deal with some of the issues relevant to the process of growing up. Parents want to give their best to their offspring- their love, affection, facilities, material comforts, opportunities to learn new things, but they do not want to lose control. The question of where to draw lines poses a big challenge to them. Some of the major issues like, how much discipline to demand, what information about sexuality and mixing up with the opposite sex is to be given at what stage, how to help them develop their confidence and how to deal with the growing up processes leave them confused and in need of informed discussion. The development of assets and challenges is an ongoing phenomenon. These do not reach the end point of development at reaching the age of 19 years, indicating the possibility of stretching the adolescence further and merging into young adulthood.

Tips for Parents

As parents have the most significant role in facilitating the process of asset development and preparing their wards to cope with the ongoing challenges, some tips are provided here:

1. **Prepare Yourself and the Adolescent.** Parents should prepare themselves and their ward to deal with the numerous changes occurring in the body coupled with emotional and psychological changes, as many of them may not understand what is happening to them. They should discuss with their adolescent the changes that take place during puberty, even before these occur.

2. **Allow Reasonable Amount of Privacy to your Adolescent.** Accept it as natural that all adolescents require privacy in which to contemplate about changes taking place in

them. They need some personal and physical space of their own to introspect, feel and form opinions.

3. Different Domains are Interrelated. Parents should realize that the assets and challenges in one dimension are related to those in other dimensions. The assets and challenges in physical and emotional domain do affect those in cognitive domain and thus the schoolwork. The adolescent may worry about self development, or about what is going on at home and then may not find it possible to concentrate in studies.

4. Concern over Identity. The adolescents' quest for independence is normal. Parents need not be over concerned about it and consider it a point of rejection or a loss of control. Help them by remaining a consistent figure without dominating or overtaking her/his emerging independent identity.

5. Accept Challenge to Your Authority. Parents and in most cases the fathers find it difficult to take that their adolescent dares to challenge their authority. They may resort to punitive action and begin to suspect them in being wrong company, while adolescents may still be respecting them. They should accept that the power struggles come up when authority is at stake/or "being right" becomes the primary issue. Ultimately, one of the parties (typically the teen) is overpowered, causing her/him to lose face, melt down and activating feelings of embarrassment, inadequacy, resentment, and bitterness.

6. Give Adolescents Information and Guidance. Teens need information and guidance at each step of growing up, as they are confused by the rapidity as well as multiplicity of changes occurring in every sphere of their life. The lack of information may make them go through numerous uncertainties, lose self-confidence and getting trapped into wrong situations.

2

Body Image

The hardest challenge is to be yourself in a world where everyone is trying to make you be somebody else.

E.E. Cummings

All children are beautiful. Parents and others around should see them as beautiful and wish them well in future. The focus should be on the qualities they have and how can these be developed further. The teens should thus acquire the ability to appreciate their unique qualities and looks, and see themselves having a good body image.

Concern for Body Image

Body image is a person's inner notion of her/his physical appearance. It suggests to the person how attractive one looks to outsiders as it presents to them the basis of forming their first impression about her/him. It sets in motion a chain of ideas about the person, namely, the physical features, way of presentation, sensitivity to the context etc. If a person is pleased with her/his body shape, appearance, dressing, hair styles, and presentation one develops positive self-image and leads to 'I am O.K. feeling', whereas a negative body image may make one feel depressed. Adolescents are in search of self-identity and get overly concerned about their looks, thinking it to be the reflection of their personality. It is their primary asset and the source of recognition in the absence of other qualities (talent in an area, hobbies etc.). In fact, the desire to have a good body image is normal to persons in all age groups. Most adults when they have visitors or are going out take good care of selecting their clothes, hair styles, shoes, etc. and the way they would wear them and meet them. The desire to have a good body image is truly great in adolescents as they are making their entry into the world they visualize as their own and that would give them positive self-esteem in years to come. They intensely search for body images that they may find outstandingly attractive, appealing and ideal in their world view, and they can maintain it as their desired goal for now and in coming years. How do adolescents conceptualize and define body image ideals and make subsequent self-comparisons on the timescale are important to know for them and others? These definitions reflect their perspectives and personal standards, which may be strongly influenced by their personal, familial, and cultural factors (both covert and overt). The hightened concern of adolescents about their body image may be attributed to three possible reasons :

1. A discrepancy between the perceptions of adolescents and the socially valued body figure: They perceive themselves to be different than the social norms and like to attain a body image that is more conforming to their own as well as expectations of others. The reactions of others, like-'mom says that I am fat', 'so and so has a perfect figure', 'you must do some exercise', 'you must work to improve your skin', heightens the concern about body image. The discrepancy may also arise from adolescents' self-driven need to look more attractive or the socially held views that 'boys like slim girls' that they do things related to self-preoccupation. The prevalent higher consciousness of schooled adolescents about their body image may be reflecting their awareness to improve themselves to some extent.
2. The influence of media and the prevalent cultural expectations on their thinking processes: They see in the media what is prized socially and desire to reach those levels as desired indicators of success. The teens see the body images of models, stars and other celebrities portrayed in news, magazines, movies,

fashion shows and music videos and try to imitate them. They carry in their minds an image of a physically perfect person they like and compare themselves against it. They like to dress and behave like them. Various advertisements used to promote the products, like soaps, creams, shampoos etc. also convey that fair and flawless complexion, long and silky hair, and slim body are the perfect body images.

3. The genetic and biological vulnerability of each person to attain certain levels of development: For example, most have an inherited predisposition to gain certain height and weight, irrespective of food and physical exercise. Children born to obese parents have higher probability to become obese in early years itself and more so at puberty.

The teens are displaying nowadays a visible and action-focused concern about body image as they even try to alter their figures. It is seen in the number of trips they make to gyms, physical fitness centres and beauty parlours etc. Many image consultants have reported that in last five years there has been a tremendous uptrend of youngsters coming for an image makeover. They believe that making an appealing impression is many times more important than being well-qualified for a competitive assignment. Intellectual functioning and academic excellence have taken a back seat. While it is extremely difficult for most teens to look like their models in life, they do not want to leave any stone unturned that can help them change or at least improve their looks. It is found that the internalization of body image, peer criticism about appearance, and knowledge of Body Mass Index (BMI) can directly contribute to body dissatisfaction. Some parents and teachers have been concerned about the high focus of their growing adolescents on self image, and if they should support that attitude. It is felt that the adults should try to help the adolescents attain a good body image and make them feel more confident, but should also instill such attitudes that would do away their misconceptions.

Some differences are noted between adolescent boys and girls in the importance they attach to the internalization of the body image and appearance culture. The contemporary trend in body images/styles continues of being thin, tall and having muscular looks exemplified many times in their choice of stars. Girls desire to look slim, pretty and curved. They are taken by looks of stars like Aishwarya, Priyanka, and Angelina, and undergo weight loss to the point of suffering from eating disorders. The practice of taking proteins and steroids among girls is not very common at this time, but if taken it can be dangerous. In boys, masculinity shows a new trend as boys are showing high vulnerability to body dissatisfaction. They are trying to look like Hrithik, SRK, John and Salman. Boys aspire to develop taut and bulging biceps, beefcake muscles and six-pack abs, and are ready to pay a high price. They derive their inspiration from action toys sold in markets and the onslaught of media on images that glamourize the muscular fit boys and heroes on the big screen.

The development of a perfect body image is not easy to attain as it requires many years to develop. Teens do not have the patience to work for long time and wait for results. They become focused on cosmetic modifications, like changing clothing types, habits of grooming, hairdo styles etc. Some rich ones even go for medical interventions. They pump in steroids and protein powder in their bodies aggressively. Some inject testerone, pop chroming, picoline or herbal stuff like Gugul and Chinese Ginseng. Some of the gym instructors report that boys are so desperate to look like models that they will eat anything you mention to them. They do not even consult a medical expert. They get frustrated and depressed in a few weeks as results are not visible that quickly.

Mihir, a 19 years old boy living next door was telling his close friend last week that he will be taking another Deca Durabolin injection tomorrow. Three days later he had to be admitted to the hospital for the treatment of kidney damage. Diwakar started taking ephedrine (a stimulant to boost his metabolism) at 17 years to fulfil his ambition of having Schwarzenegger like body. Everyone desires to look impressive, bigger and sexier, but as soon as injecting stops, the body slumps. In fact, the long-term damages may be serious as they may not attain more than 95% of the normal height they would have attained in the normal course, and may become susceptible to fits of anger such as seen in some cases of road rage.

For adolescents looking attractive remains a very important ambition and they need continued reassurance from people in their context, namely, parents, peers, teachers etc. that they look absolutely beautiful in their normal looks. If they are not encouraged to think positively, they may begin using variety of cosmetics being influenced by the advertisements of what will make them look beautiful. There is demand for brand clothes in the hope that these would help them look smarter and attractive. Particularly in girls it is reported that they like to wear clothes similar to those used by celebrities, which may at times violate their personal and social norms. An adolescent is said to have negative body image when s/he begins to overemphasise the negative aspects of the body over the positive characteristics. This leads to low self-esteem leading to many complexes and unwanted behaviours. When adolescents in schools become over involved in their body image change, it becomes problematic to their concentration on studies, eating patterns, social relationships and normal functioning expected of their age and thus a cause of concern for parents and teachers.

Aspects of Concern

Some concerns related to aspects of body image have been identified on the basis of data obtained from school going adolescent girls and boys in Classes IX, X and XI during some counseling sessions on physical appearance. Students were handed small slips of paper to write their body concerns and what they do to attain these, and then drop the slips in the box kept near the door without writing their names. These were then read and separated for girls and boys. The counselor identified those showing some excessive concern and met them personally. Some cases are discussed here with names changed.

Concerns of Girls

Looks. Mita, an 11 years old girl studying in class VI, is always sitting on the back seat in the class and staring at other girls she considers prettier than herself. She often tries to find out from them what they do to look pretty. At home she tends to hide in a bedroom whenever any guest would come in the house. She keeps on sitting in front of the mirror for long time, looking at her face from different angles. She puts face cream and powder on her cheeks and arms. She would add more and more, rub it off and put again, repeating the process several times. Once done what she can do to her face maximally, she would go and tell her mother 'I have now become like Geeta, so do not scold me anymore.' Her older sister Geeta is a fair complexioned girl. Mita hears her relatives making constant remarks to her parents 'Who does your Mita look like? All of you in the family have quite fair complexion but her.' Days in and days out, Mita continues to sit in front of the mirror for long time and ponders about the use of different cosmetics to improve her complexion. She tries every day something new with no results and is at times very dissatisfied and angry with herself, her siblings and mother. After a few months, she suddenly stopped talking to other girls in the class, who she considered prettier than herself. She would complain against them to the teacher without any reason.

Similar to Mita many other girls in their developing teens may display higher consciousness about their features, complexion, height and weight they think is not in conformity to what they wish to have. A poor body image tends to lead to inferiority complex and negative behaviours, such as shyness, anger, aggression, back biting etc.

In contrast to the above, when a mother saw her daughter frequently rubbing powder on her face and arms and saying 'now I have also become fair like you', she reminded her of Sneha Aunty a dark complexioned neighbour, who was appreciated and liked by everybody because of her helping nature and charming personality. Sensing her daughter's high concern about the physical self, she often talked to her about some of the famous people (Mother Teresa, Lal Bahadur

Shastri etc.), who did not have a good body image but still became famous because of their talents. She also started pointing out the positive qualities of her daughter and gave her opportunities to develop her talents. Soon the daughter started displaying higher self-confidence.

Clothing. Girls take great interest in the choice of clothes. They become the focus of attention of others when they over indulge in styles and express constant dissatisfaction with whatever they have or can have.

Shreya, a class IX student plan to go to a friend's birthday party. She is in her room trying different outfits she has, one after another, standing in front of the mirror. She is there for nearly two hours and still not done. She comes out of the room with a swollen face to the mother that she has nothing to wear for the party. She insists that mother should take her out for shopping for a new outfit. The mother refused as she can not understand Shreya's behaviour. Shreya called a couple of other friends and found all having the same tale.

Such behaviours put financial strain on families and cause tension (particularly on not so rich families). One mother commented 'I got the skirts made for you three months back and now you do not like to wear them. You discard the clothes so quickly like these do not cost money. How many clothes do you buy? Where can I afford them?' The girls are constantly haggling to buy clothes, which are trendy, stylish and give more exposure to their bodies. This is irritating to many parents, particularly fathers as they want them to choose culturally appropriate styles than dress like celebrities. Even teachers tell—'The girls' skirts are getting shorter by the day. Do we have any respect left for our culture?'

A little more patience is required to deal with the adolescents. Some freedom may be given for experimenting with the clothes to decide what suits them though it may not be ideal from an adult's eye. Limits may be set in terms of what is acceptable in the socio-cultural environment. Appreciation and praise will enhance their confidence and self-image. Girls do listen to their mother if they have a loving relationship.

A counselor observed: A group of students of Class XII announced a party before the Board exams. Although the party was still five weeks away, the girls were already getting together in groups talking about it. They were discussing constantly about their clothes despite the heavy burden of studies on their heads during that period. They looked at the schedules when they could be out on shopping sprees, as it could not be done in one go. They had to look around, tryout, and match accessories and jewellery and what not. A large number of such girls got together in the group. Some of them made telephone calls to their seniors and relatives to find out if they could lend them some things, like matching shoes, accessories and bags. On the day of the party, it was a scene to look at them from morning itself. They were more anxious than happy. There was a bee line since afternoon on parlours for hair styling, waxing and other things. Face packs were put on faces in the evening. Hours were spent on dressing up, styling, rehearsing and what not. At about 7.00 p.m. finally they left the room. The room was in a condition as if a tornado has just passed over it, leaving behind heaps of clothes tried but not worn and dumped like garbage, half of them half opened and spread around. They all wanted to wear what was in fashion and what were used by persons in media and celebrities. Many of them were caught up in the tussle between what they wanted to wear and what the mothers will approve. A mother who went to drop the girls at the venue said that girls came in such a variety of dresses-long dresses, short dresses, salwar kamiz, ethnic wears and even western dresses, and wondered about the adolescent world.

Having a Body Like Others. Preeti a class VIII student has been quite worried about her developing body. Several times she was seen coaxing her friend to ask the counselor some questions on her behalf. When the counselor asked her if she wanted to ask something, she kept saying 'no'. The counselor then asked her friend to find out if she wanted to know something. Her friend then came back and told 'Ma'am Preeti is very concerned about her body. She is 14-1/2 years and her breasts have not developed much, whereas her most classmates have developed quite well. She is worried if there was something wrong with her and/or if she needs to consult a doctor.'

The counselor reassured that there was nothing wrong with her. She was a lean and thin girl. Some girls develop later than others. There are individual differences in the time of development, and the growth pattern is different in different people. As all of us have different height, complexion and features from each other, similarly the time of development of breasts can also be different in different girls. However, if girls do not start to develop breasts or menstruate till the age of 16, parents should consult a doctor. She also explained from the reverse angle. She said that a 10 or 11 years old girl also may feel very self-conscious if she has early breast development. She may feel very awkward. Girls then require a different set of clothes, which will make them feel less awkward and more self- confident.

Hair on Face. A student shared a friend's feelings with the school counselor: Both boys and girls, in Class X were very excited about the plan of having a get together at one of the class fellows' house after the Board exams. Girls started jumping right away on the idea of party. They began planning the arrangements—how they will go, who will pick up whom and what they will wear. Richa a quiet girl seemed somewhat unsure about her ability to join the group and go to the party. As the clock was ticking, in the evening she rang up her friend Shashi to say that she will not be able to come for the get together. She was very upset but not telling the reasons. On probing for long she confessed that 'I have a lot of hair on my upper lip and face. My mother has been bed-ridden for quite some time. I don't have anybody to help me. I also do not have enough money on me. I am in no situation to tell my mother to take me to a parlour. What do I do? I have no choice but to stay at home. I am very upset and have not even taken lunch. I will not be able to study either.'

Adolescent girls may become very conscious of the facial hair as it signifies manly features, and may need help.

Stooping. Shivani a 12½ years old girl has started stooping this term while walking. She attained puberty when she was a little less than 12 years. She has a healthy physique and seems to be well developed for her age. She has gained lot of height in past six months, which has made her look taller than other girls in the class. In fact, she is taller than some boys too. The clothes that she was fond of wearing six months back, she feel look awkward now. She keeps repeatedly wearing some dresses in which her developing body does not show. She still has a liking for her body image she had at ten or so.

Shivani had not been conscious of the gradual changes happening in her body so far. She used to be a playful girl and liked by her friends. Other girls in her playgroup at home have not changed much, but at school some have changed and others are still growing. She thus fails to place herself comfortably among others. She is also not able to handle her growing body. She does not know how best to carry herself. She is shy about her growing body symbolizing an adult shape. She has become very self-conscious and started stooping so that her body does not show much.

Shivani is quite lucky to have a mother who is quite sensitive to the needs of her growing up. On noticing her daughter stooping, she decided to have a talk with her. She took the daughter to her little garden and showed her a flower bed. She picked up a small flower and a fully bloomed flower and asked her to compare and tell which one looked prettier. Obviously the girl answered in favour of the fully bloomed flower. The mother told that like this flower the fully grown body looked much prettier. Though she had told the girl about many internal and external changes occurring in the body during puberty, she repeated those to her. She reassured the girl that breast development was a natural and normal aspect of female growing up. Nature prepares a girl for future so that when she gets married and has a child she can nurse her baby. One day Shivani found that her mother has replaced some of her clothes with new but less expensive items. First she was upset but then she quietly tried them. On trying she was amazed that these outfits were more suitable for a growing teenage girl like her and can be purchased in small budget. Very soon, Shivani regained her confidence and started talking about her own body. She was able to accept herself easily and also share her problems with her mother.

Weight. Quite a number of girls reported that they are fat and this makes them very self-conscious. They feel others look down upon them as they are not in shape. They try to live on salad and fruit diets for days to lose weight. They generally have diet cokes and diet chips, whereas others take the normal ones. Very often they feel weak and having no stamina to carry out school activities. Parents and teachers observed that some girls in order to attain ideal figure resort to extreme diet schedules. They also join weight loss programmes.

It thus appears that the main body image concerns of girls are looks (features, complexion), clothing, having a body like others (size of breasts, excessive hair on face and body), hairdo, ability to carry oneself, weight and acne/pimples.

Pimples. Pimples was in fact an area of concern for girls as well as boys. About pimples many of the girls wrote: 'I am worried about my face. I get lot of pimples. It is not only painful, it causes me embarrassment. I am always thinking that other people must be looking at my face, and telling how ugly I look? I feel very self-conscious. I have tried many anti-pimple creams and medicines. I have even tried homeopathy medicines. I keep washing my face many a times during the day, but nothing helps. I understand that fried and oily food causes pimples. I have stopped eating fried food, but still I get lot of pimples. Some people tell me pimples are due to impure blood. What should I do to get my blood purified? Not only me, also my parents are quite worried.'

Some of the boys also found pimples equally painful but made more positive comments. Some wrote: 'I have girlish skin because I have pimples,' 'Some people say pimples come out because I have sexual urges. I have no answer to such questions as I don't feel anything at the moment, except the hurt.'

Concerns of Boys

Height & Weight. 15 years old Saurabh is a very thin and short looking boy. He has not gained much height so far whereas other boys and girls have become quite tall. He remains very worried. He is also upset as often he is called 'Liliput' by his friends. His behaviour has become a cause of concern as he would remain sitting quietly by himself, not bothering even to raise his hand in the class when taking a count for participation in various activities. On the contrary, he felt at times upset why other children raise their hands fast and run for participating in the activities. Gradually it turned out that he is not even noticed by many of the teachers. He would shirk from participating in all kinds of school activities. His facial expression has also started to look dull and emotionally disturbed.

Hairs Styling. A mother counted that her son Mohit combed his hairs 70 times in a day till he got the hair style he wanted. She did not understand why her son does this and commented: 'How much time do you waste on doing this. You have many important things to do at this age. There is so much competition in all fields. You need to spend time and energy somewhere else.'

Mrs. Wanshu, the principal was taking a round in the school when she noticed that three boys of class XI have just seen her and turned their back on her. She noticed that all of them have got their haircut very small almost like a clean shave. On asking they said that they were very scared of her scolding them. They just could not believe their ears but smiled when the principal said: 'You must be feeling very cool with this new hair style. I like it.' They were very happy and went for the class. They felt that the principal realized their need for recognition.

Similar to these are many boys having hair cuts in different styles from mushroom cut, having spikes to keeping a pony tail behind. Some get their hairs totally shaved off. They do all this in search of a new identity or their desire to be noticed by others or to seek attention. Adults need not get worked up as it is a temporary phase and gradually they will settle down.

Ability to Carry Oneself. Rohan, a 15½ years old boy has become more or less a withdrawn child coming to class X. He feels very awkward with himself. He doesn't know how to carry himself in front of people. Every few months he is becoming taller whereas till a year earlier he was a small boy in the house pampered by everybody. In two years he has grown to become 5'11" tall. His voice has started to crack. People in the family often joke that what is wrong with his voice and mimic him. Fringes of hair have started appearing on his face. The role expectations by the adults around have changed tremendously. The clothes he used to wear six months ago have gone short and look funny on him. Parents force him to wear some of those clothes but he is not happy to do so. On top of all this his mother hanged up all his expensive clothes for future use as she says she could not afford to buy them every six months. Mother also has the habit of checking him a lot. Almost 10 times in a day she would check him—'walk properly, eat properly.' He was expected to wish the guests visiting them in a certain manner.

Rohan has not developed any hobbies to keep himself involved and busy. His extra focus on his body made him feel awkward. He had good deal of pressure of studies as he was in class X and has to take Board exams. His parents nagged him a lot for high performance. All this made him very unsure of himself. He would often lock himself in his room for long hours. His socialization was adversely affected. He even started avoiding to converse with his family members. He would get irritated on small issues. Whenever his cousins etc. came he would feel odd with them and felt he had nothing to talk to.

When the class teacher referred him to the counselor, she found it initially difficult to make the boy open up. He was given lot of reassurance and helped in gaining self-confidence. She also advised parents not to make Rohan self-conscious with negative comments. Parents should be supportive of children at this age rather than being critical; lest the child starts feeling something is gravely wrong. There should be no emphasis on having expensive clothes. Rather parents should help Rohan to choose the clothes in which he looks nice and comfortable. They should also avoid putting over emphasis on studies, as it leads to stress and lower performance.

The main body image concerns of boys appeared to be weight and height, hair styles, and being able to handle their growing body.

Summing Up

Apparently the teenager girls and boys are quite concerned about their looks, dressing up and grooming. They are self-conscious of their weight, hair styles, clothes, shoes and accessories. They spend hours thinking about these and discussing with friends. They are very concerned about their self-image. They are over sensitive to any comment/remark about their appearance from others which are not congruent to what they think.

While it is true that their concerns are genuine and they want to make an effort to enhance their body image. Looking physically attractive gives them a boost in society, how they are accepted and how they accept or reject themselves. A positive body image thus becomes important for adolescents in search of self-identity. A positive image enhances one's self-confidence, while a negative body image tends to produce an inferiority complex, anxiety, depression, irritation and withdrawal from society. There are many adolescents who suffer from a negative body image and over indulgence with their looks. Some body concern during adolescence is normal as all teens want to look good. But if obsessed with themselves they may adopt some socially unacceptable ways to get the attention of others. Many young boys and girls start smoking, drinking and consuming drugs in order to enhance the body image. They also indulge in unprotected sex to seek attention of opposite sex. They can be guided at an early age to take up some hobbies or develop interest in other activities as means of getting recognition.

Tips for Parents and Teachers

Teachers and parents can be very helpful in enhancing the self-image of adolescents.

1. Not Ridiculing. Do not ridicule the adolescent about body image. Instead of focusing on the physical characteristics, highlight their positive personality characteristics, their nature, interests, helpfulness, hardworking, courage etc. as white skin is not always beautiful. De-emphasize the colour of the skin.

2. Appreciate Natural Looks. Appreciate the attributes and qualities your ward has to make her/him feel good. Do not make negative remarks about weight, body hairs etc.

3. Help Accept Natural Changes. Help adolescents accept and take pride in their developing bodies for which many are not prepared. As pimples are considered a problem both by girls and boys, the parents and counselors should communicate to them clearly that many teenagers get pimples or acne due to the hormonal changes during puberty. One should not worry about them as they vanish on their own with age. It is not related to a particular diet. However, a diet rich in fruits and salads is better than oily food.

4. Develop Hobbies. Parents should give them opportunities to develop hobbies and interests so that they feel proud of their strengths, like achievements in music, arts, reading etc.

5. Help Know One's Qualities. Teacher should ask periodically each adolescent to enumerate her/his strengths, the physical and personality characteristics.

6. Discuss Qualities of Chosen Icons. As adolescents generally copy celebrities and other famous people ask them to pick up from time to time names and characteristics of such people. Discuss the personality qualities of personalities like Kalpana Chawla, Mother Teresa, and Lal Bahadur Shashtri etc. who did not have highly rated physical appearances, yet rose to fame because of their other strengths.

Tips for Adolescents

1. **Overdoing is Unnecessary.** It is perfectly O.K. to look at own body, but do not overdo it to the point it becomes an obsession.

2. **Avoid Over Concern.** Over concern for body image can have negative effects on one's ability to think and engage in creative endeavour. Rima has been dieting so hard for past couple of months that all the time she counts calories, carb and fat contents of the food she eats. She now eats only a serving of salads at lunch and dinner time. She looks anemic, and shows symptoms of anorexia nervosa.

3. **Cleanliness is Important.** Keeping the skin clean and grooming of body are important in all age groups and particularly for adolescents.

4. **Sparing Use of Cosmetics.** Those prone to get pimples should avoid cosmetics on the skin as these further clog the pores. Do not prick with nails. Wash the face with soap and water 2-3 times a day. Do not be oversensitive about your looks. Your friends like meeting you. They do not look at your pimples.

5. **Emphasis on Carrying Self.** Put more emphasis on neatly dressing up, good mannerism, correct posture and way of walking. Smita and Tanuj always felt the way you carry yourself is the important thing for your body image.

6. **Ideal Image not the Only Goal.** Remember not to over indulge in achieving an ideal body image as you may end up wasting lot of time and money on cosmetics, clothes and gyms with no future direction or gains. Swati rushes every month in search of new creams and skin aids in addition to increase her workout time but finds no weight loss.

7. **Avoid being At-Risk.** Adolescents should not indulge in risk taking behaviours to enhance their self-image. Suresh resorted to wearing tight clothes and smoking cigarettes to impress his friends but suffered from bouts of asthma.

3

Eating Habits

Appetite comes with eating.

Francois Rabelais

After the PTA meeting some teachers told the counselor that many of the parents they met were concerned about the eating habits of their adolescents. They seemed to have frequent trouble on the dinner table with constant bickering and tempers about the food items prepared, type of food and the schedule of eating. Adolescents preferred to have food different than rest of the family. They want to eat at different timings and are not bothered about the quality of food. They are not happy about the food schedules parents have set. They are complaining about the home cooked food and are keen on having different fancy food items on the shelves in the market and/or sold at eating jaunts/restaurants. Parents find it difficult to convince them of the need of consuming healthy foods rich in protein, vitamins, iron and fibers as they are going through the phase of rapid physical and cognitive development. Parents want their wards to attain their maximum potential growth free of illness and are at wits end.

Forming of Eating Habits

Eating habits are inculcated in the child over time since birth. In each family, the child is fed culturally appropriate and healthy food items at certain timings. Most parents like to see that the children eat at right time, eat healthy food and eat well to maintain their good health. For young school children in general, it is a common family practice that in the morning they take some milk and cereal prior to going to school and carry some 'tiffin' to eat at school during recess. They have lunch after they come back home, have some milk and snacks in the evening, and the dinner at night. As the children come close to puberty they try to assert themselves to exercise preference for what to eat and when. They avoid eating any breakfast prior to going to school and do not maintain regularity in meals. Girls in particular become over concerned about their figure and avoid eating healthy food and with regularity. The adolescents' eating habits and the need of eating nutritious food are the concerns of parents and teachers as well.

No Breakfast

Ritika, a sweet and delicate looking student of class VII, who came to school a few minutes ago, fainted while the school assembly was in progress. Two children picked her up and brought her to the school medical room. She was given glucose and the required medical aid by the medical in-charge. She regained consciousness after a while. She was then asked by the medical in-charge, 'did you eat/drink anything in the morning before coming to the school.' Ritika's reply was, 'No.' Again she was asked, 'Why?' Ritika said, 'I do not feel like eating in the morning.' She was given some biscuits and tea in the medical room. After some time she was sent back to the classroom.

Like this, in summer time, there are quite a few children who are seen fainting during school assembly in the morning time or on the playground. The school counselors have reported the feeling of discomfort about children coming to school without having breakfast. They have tried to bring the issue for discussion with parents during the P.T.A. meetings in the school. They have not found the parents having any less concern. Every day they had to listen to- 'you don't tell me', 'you don't know', 'I do not feel like eating' and so on. Parents were fed up of listening to, 'I don't feel hungry', 'No body takes tiffin to the school', 'I will eat samosa/bread pakora in the school'. The mothers complained that they try to do their best yet in vain. They get up early in the morning to prepare the lunch boxes but children either deliberately leave the boxes behind or many times do not eat it. The parents have expressed their frustration on account of adolescents' attitudes towards eating. They want, in fact, the help of the counselor/school to resolve this problem so as not to find their children suffering from eating problems of any kind. On the other hand, in some of the poor families, it is noticed that mothers do not bother about their children eating something before leaving for school or if they carry any tiffin with them.

The eating habits of adolescents have also been disturbing to teachers as when a student fell sick in the class it was their responsibility to take care of them. Many teachers complained that a good number of students come to the school without having milk or any breakfast. As a result most of the time, in the morning itself, students are not fresh and bright looking. They are not excited at all about schoolwork. The habit of not eating in the morning assumes serious dimensions during adolescence as now they develop an attitude to push the barriers for most things. The counselors have often talked to the adolescents about the importance of nutritious food in their growing up and also its relation to the school performance at this stage. Adolescent responses have been quite varied though.

Multiple Activities

It has been observed that adolescents are becoming increasingly careless about eating because of the pressure to participate in other activities/hobbies, tuitions etc. At this stage there is lot of pressure of studies and also the need to excel in other spheres. The adolescent has to live up to the expectations of the parent and achieve in a competitive world making food often the last priority.

Anuradha is a student in class X. She is a conscientious student but very careless about her diet. She leaves for the school bus at 6.30 a.m. in the morning after having a little milk, as she does not like to eat anything early in the morning. She carries one sandwich with her which she takes during lunch break. Many times she misses that too as she always has to do some extra work or has to ask the teachers something. Straight from school she goes for her math tuition and returns home after 4.00 o'clock. After coming home she takes some food, rests for a while and again sits for studies. By evening she gets so tired that she fails to concentrate on anything. She continues to repeat without understanding anything and gets headaches. She again sits to complete her home work after dinner. She keeps on drinking coffee to remain awake. She makes mistakes and repeats the work. All the time she is unhappy and kind of depressed that she is not able to meet her desired goals. Her mother is a working woman and is not able to be around all the time to look after her needs. In fact the parents are stressed with their own work demands. They see her working hard and feel satisfied that their daughter is trying to do her best in studies. They however, do not pay much attention to her dietary habit and headaches.

One day Anuradha blacked out in the school field and was brought to the counselor. The counselor found out that she was a good student and has understanding parents. She checked her routine and noted that she was not eating properly and was overworking to satisfy the higher expectations of parents. She needed time to relax, do some physical exercise and have a proper diet. She needed to take nutritious food including fruits and vegetables. In the evening she should take a glass of milk with bournvita instead of coffee.

Similar to Anuradha there are a number of adolescents who are worked up with their studies, are busy running from one activity to the other and have no emphasis on their diet. Relaxation of mind and body, and proper sleep hours are equally important for adolescents.

A common observation of parents and teachers has been that many of the young girls and boys between 13 to 20 years are over concerned about their looks and body image. They knowingly deprive themselves of food and turn anemic. On the other hand obesity is also on the increase among some adolescents because of consuming fancy and high carbohydrate foods.

Anemia

Stuti, a 16 years old girl belonged to a conservative joint family living with other male cousins in the same household. Her mother was always preoccupied in some family affair though she was not a working woman. She hardly talked to Stuti and Stuti did not share her personal problems with her mother. Lately, Stuti's friends and teachers noticed that she remained lethargic and felt very sleepy even during the day. In class she remained dull and inactive. She was earlier fond of sports but now would prefer to sit on the playground instead of playing. The games teacher called her in the field one day and asked if there was some particular reason for not participating in games. While talking to her the game teacher noticed that Stuti looked very pale. She took her hand and noticed that even her nails were quite pale instead of pink. The teacher then asked about her menstrual cycle, if she has bleeding for more than 4-5 days. Stuti broke down and after some time told the teacher that she was having very heavy bleeding during her periods every time and it lasts for nearly a week.

Stuti was advised to talk to her mother and seek medical advice. She was recommended iron supplements and consuming more foods rich in iron, such as jaggery, nuts, leafy green vegetables and fruits as amla, guava, citrus fruits, spinach, and meat.

Obesity

While some students are not eating enough, some others are eating wrong foods. They are consuming calorie rich foods having too much of carbohydrates and fats and thus gain excessive weight.

Sandy (Sandeep) has been a pampered boy in the family. He is known to get his way with parents for everything right from his childhood. He goes out with parents in the evenings after they come back from work, to numerous eating joints. He makes fuss about every food item parents order, and ultimately overeats one such item that he likes. As Sandy grew older, all the time he demanded to eat out and developed the habit of feeding himself on fast food. If the mother rang up from her office to find out if he has had lunch, he answered "No, I don't like to eat the food made at home and I have ordered a big pizza for myself." His after lunch routine was to sleep and then in the evening to watch T.V. play some latest electronic game or sit in front of the computer. All this while he would polish whole packet of chips and a large bottle of Pepsi or at times would force the maid to fry finger chips in large quantities.

Sandy's mother has been a choosy eater herself and did not mind this habit initially thinking that at least the boy was eating something. Many times for dinner either he was not hungry as he took heavy snacks in the evening or he would only eat eggs and parathas with lot of butter on it or some fast food again. He did not like to eat the vegetables and fruits. As a result he had put on lot of weight and developed double chin by the time he reached class IX.

After the first term he started complaining of strain and pain in bones and knee-joints. He was not able to run much. On medical referral he was diagnosed of calcium deficiency, besides certain other problems. He was advised to have at least two glasses of milk every day and to give up colas altogether. A more balanced diet with green vegetables and fruit was recommended. He was advised to undertake regular physical exercise to reduce weight as it was putting pressure on the knees.

The counselors observed that in general there was a high tendency among youngsters to have pizza, burger, noodles and similar food. Another lot of students who are not able to afford the expensive foodstuff prefer to eat chat, papri, samosas, but not regular food. A large part of students' diet includes such stuff having high carbohydrates and fat content, and no fruits and vegetables. Along with the developing of wrong eating habits children are living with changes in their life styles. The daily routines of adolescents have no time provision/emphasis on physical exercise or playing outdoor games and sports. Even parents give very little importance to this as compared to other activities especially when the children enter their teens. It happens more in case of girls as parents do not encourage them for any physical exercise. Children of all ages need to do physical exercise or play in order to have a healthy body and to develop good appetite. Playing outdoors for at least one hour is very essential.

A 15 years old girl Anjali thought that she was obese and hung herself in despair. Rita Mishra started remaining on a diet of Diet Coke, corn and other low calorie snacks and then only on bowls of salads for weeks. Ridhima had severe nutritional deficiency which led to her hair falling off, irregular menstrual cycle and getting tired very soon. This was because of the killer combination of wrong eating habits. There are teenagers who are scared of getting jeers on 'fat legs' and/or 'big tummies'. Girls desire to be thin, but not curvaceous. Some are willing to go as far as to have Lipoplasty or a Liposuction. They want to be thin fast. They are more or less living in a delusional world where anyone and everyone can be slim like a model.

During adolescence, girls are challenged to come to terms with the physical changes of puberty, including considerable weight gain. As adolescent girls attempt to reconcile the reality of their bodies with the unrealistic demands for female thinness, a large number of girls experience intense body image dissatisfaction. For some girls, negative feelings about their bodies and their efforts to achieve or maintain thinness contribute to the development of disordered eating habits. This may include binge eating, restrictive dieting, or induced vomiting and overeating, leading to more serious disorders.

Eating Disorders

Eating difficulties if left unattended may take pathological roots and can become eating disorder. Eating disorders are known to be complex in nature and affect adolescents with increasing frequency. These rank indeed as the third most common chronic health problem in adolescents, particularly the females. Two commonly known eating disorders affecting adolescents are anorexia nervosa and bulimia nervosa.

Anorexia Nervosa

Anorexia nervosa or self-starvation, is a common problem among teenage girls. It is a condition of eating where the person restricts food intake to a minimum. It is diagnosed as a disorder when a person weighs 15% less than the expected on the growth charts. This is caused by a psychological condition in which the adolescent has fears about gaining weight, has an unrealistic image of her body and suffers from a possible loss or interruption of her menstrual cycle. After some time the body refuses to accept more food.

Sujata an 18 years old student from a private school has joined lately, a reputed women's college. She had been very excited about going to the college as she has been looking forward to this. To begin with she found it a novel experience, a sudden freedom in her routine, dressing up and meeting new friends, and overall getting rid of the practice of carrying the tiffin. In a couple of weeks she began to take the senior girls as her role models. After the passage of four months in the first year of college, she had in her the strong need of being noticed in the group. She felt that she may quickly do it by giving herself a pet name. She thus chose Suzi as her name to be used by her friends instead of Sujata. Her dressing up became trendy, and her eating patterns changed. She stopped carrying tiffin to the college. When her parents asked 'No body takes tiffin to the college' became her curt reply to them. She would go to the college canteen in between her classes and have snacks like Samosa/Pakora or just tea. Pepsi became her new fad. In the limited pocket money she got from her parents she managed to have tea only some days, and some fast foodstuff on other days to sustain herself till 4.30 p.m., the time when she came home. She began to notice changes in her figure after the first term, and became quite thin by the end of first year of college. Her mother noticed that she has lost lot of weight and tried to talk to her about proper food, but of no avail. Sujata though happy with her slimmer body suffered now from frequent headaches, stomachache, dizziness and was not able to concentrate on studies. She felt very happy and proud of herself when she got compliments from her peers and classmates- 'you have a sexy figure', 'you are very slim'. Gradually she became so thin that she looked sick. Some family friends and relatives started telling her parents 'Sujata looks sick. We hope there is nothing wrong with her.' She started to have white patches on her face. Her natural charm was gone. One day suddenly she blacked out on the bus stand. On coming home she reported it to her parents. They took her for a medical checkup. She was recommended some counseling in addition to changes in food regimen.

The counselor, parents and the family doctor repeatedly discussed the issue with her for a couple of months to convince her about the need of nutritious food during adolescence. She then committed to increase her intake gradually till she reached the point of the prescribed diet. To start with she had more fruits and salads which helped in increasing her appetite and yet did not make her feel uncomfortable. Then she began eating breakfast and carried tiffin to the college, in addition to spending her pocket money.

Bulimia Nervosa

It is seen in the tendency of adolescents to eat large amounts of food followed by behaviours to eliminate the food, such as resorting to vomiting, fasting, use of laxatives or indulgence into excessive workouts/exercises on a frequent basis.

Helen is in class XI and an above average student. As both of her parents work, she has been very frequently eating fast foods, like potato chips, burgers etc. She eats larger quantities of these and proudly says that her growing body needs more food. Her clothes are becoming tighter every time she gets them adjusted. She looks fat indeed and is getting conscious of that. One of her friends told her recently to go to gym regularly and eat less. Helen has strong urge for food and can not stop herself from eating. Then she read in a magazine that if she will take laxatives off and on it will be helpful. It has become now a habit to eat but then take laxative and get the food out of her system on a regular basis. When her parents noticed it they were upset as they find it disgusting to eat and then throw up every time. They decided to seek professional advice. The counselor chose to talk to Helen on the issue. She talked to Helen regularly and set a food and activity schedule for her. It included when, what and how much to eat and then an activity to busy herself over the week. She was advised to include in her food more of salads and fruits so that she feels full and yet does not have the urge to eat frequently. She was also asked to space out her meals and to eat popcorn and other non fried stuff if at all she needed to eat in between the meals. Helen agreed to follow the set schedule. With serious efforts of the parents, counselor and her own, Helen reached a point where she is eating normally. She has also lost about 3 kg of weight. This makes her and parents happy.

Both the eating disorders—anorexia nervosa and bulimia nervosa are found associated with serious biological, psychological and sociological morbidity, and significant mortality. Anorexia and Bulimia are on the rise. The attraction to cosmetic procedures is also on the increase and is getting costlier.

Other Eating Disorders

Some more serious eating disorders have been identified in recent years, such as, Orthorexia, Drunkorexia, and binge eating, which are dangerous variations of eating disorders of anorexia and bulimia. Orthorexia is seen as a lifestyle related disorder of the 21st century among those preoccupied with the purity of food, having preference for organically grown foods and drink distilled water.

Drunkorexia is a compound of anorexia or bulimia with alcohol abuse seen sometime in late adolescents or college students (more in females). These persons may starve whole day to offset the calories intake in their alcohol consumption. It may include bulimia involving behaviour like binging on food and alcohol and then purging. Many mix anorexia and bulimia as they find it glorified and reinforced by the models they consider cool and hap.

Reasons for Changed Practices

The change in eating practices is attributed to the following factors:

- There are too many distractions for the adolescents (e.g. TV, going out, friends, pursuing of hobbies) that provoke them to undermine the importance of food.
- There are more pressures and stress than they can handle (studies, going for various activities after school hours, stress of missing the school bus).
- Many lack understanding of what is really good and healthy and what is injurious to the health in the long-term and why.
- They are highly prone to the effect of advertisements in media.
- Many mothers do not give adequate time to food selection and preparation either because of their work pressures or ignorance.
- Taking of food at odd hours adversely affects the appetite and the metabolism.
- Adolescents go for taste more than the nutrition as they see their parents not objecting beyond a point and all friends do the same.
- Many mothers lack knowledge of the correct food combinations.
- Lack of physical exercise among adolescents keeps their hunger suppressed.
- Poverty in poor families takes away their right to be selective of foods.
- Gender discrimination in some families leads to giving more nutritional food to boys than girls.
- Liking for multi-cultural food is on the rise due to globalization.

Impact of Eating Habits

The current eating habits impact the adolescents in the form of:

- Poor body growth.
- Poor stamina.
- Poor understanding.

- Fatigue, depression and frequent headaches.
- Negative effects on studies, career, co-curricular activities.
- Anemia, calcium and other deficiencies.
- Poor eyesight.
- Frequent menstrual problems in girls.
- Higher susceptibility to diseases—Cold, Cough, Vomiting, Jaundice, Tuberculosis are some of the common ailments in school going teenage children.

Strategies for Improving Nutrition

1. **Parents take More Responsibility.** Changing the eating habits of the adolescents would put higher responsibility on the parents especially mothers to plan the food. They have to recognize that the adolescents eating habits have changed due to various influences in their context. The food selection and preparation requires little more creativity in the style of cooking and adaptability to variety of available food items.

2. **Give Attention to the Psychological Factors.** Mrinal does not like to try any milk product as he saw as a child his friend throwing up just after consuming curd. One day his mother ate curd sitting in front of him and encouraged him to try one spoon, which he did. As he did not fall sick he tried a little more next time.

3. **Make Menu Variable.** Bring in variety in the menu as adolescents desire change. Mrs. Soni always adds something different as a garnish to items. She also serves on some days different items like noodles and burgers and other continental food along with foods of different states.

4. **Prepare Variety of Salads.** Mrs. Saroj (a mother) makes many innovative salads. She tries to make combinations of legumes, sprouts, cheese, dry fruit, and sesame seed (Til) with vegetables such as celery leaves, carrot, tomato, onion, cucumber, cabbage, broccoli, etc.

5. **Make all Foods Part of Menu.** Make pizza, burger etc. which children are so fond of eating, a part of the weekly menu with a good helping of salads.

6. Combine Preferred and Essential Items. Moderate the quantities of foods liked by adolescents and add to those the essential nutrients in some form. Shruti, an 18 years old girl is fond of having plain Maggi noodles sometimes for dinner, but first she eats whatever vegetable is made at home and a bowl full of Dal (pulses). Mrs. Geeta Raman makes it a point to give a cup of chocolate milk to her children, when they are studying late in the night during exam time. In between the studies, if children like munching some things as stress busters, Mrs. Geeta Raman serves fruit chat, fresh fruit, popcorn, nuts and roasted snacks.

7. Add Nutrients. Add soya bean, cottage cheese, wheat porridge, milk and milk products in children's diet as these are healthy food items. Some cheaper food alternatives are nuts, resin, figs, dates, jaggery and peanuts that have lot of nutritional value. These can be pasted and added to food. Mrs. Suri is a conscientious mother. She would grate vegetables to put in khicharee, semolina, wheat porridge and pulses as she considered them essential for them.

8. Avoid Aerated Drinks. Juices, lime water mix, Panna, and milk shakes are better drinks than aerated colas. Serve them attractively in coloured glasses.

9. Involve Children in Planning. When children grew up Mrs. Suri started involving them in planning the menu. On Sundays, she would prepare the menu for the whole week with children's help and put on the fridge in the kitchen. She saw to it that besides children's liking, important nutrients were included in the diet.

10. Periodic Discussions. Have periodic family discussions on balanced diet and important nutrients of food. Mrs. Suri discussed balanced diet and the consequences in its absence.

11. Parents to Set Example. Mrs. Suri made it a point that parents themselves ate healthy food. Fruits were always part of breakfast and lunch. All types of seasonal vegetables and fruits were brought in their home.

12. Maintain Regular Timings and Togetherness. No office related talk or matters of tension should be discussed at eating time. It should not be used to lecture the kids. It is the time when along with food, parents have a chance to listen to kids' daily experiences and all family members interact together.

13. Maintain Regular Intervals. Inculcating good food habits right from early childhood helps later attitudes towards food. Mrs. Suri insisted on an interval of minimum four hours between meals.

14. Change in Menu of School Canteens. The school canteens should be asked to serve more nutritious food with variety on different days. Parents may make schools conscious on this issue.

Helping Tips

1. Talks on Food and Health. Organize periodic talks and discussions in the school for grades 6-12 on the importance of food and health during adolescence. The school counselors may be best suited for it as a part of school schedule.

2. Anemia Awareness. Make the adolescents and families aware of anemia. Hold frequent discussions on the causes and effects of anemia, the energy needs of adolescents, need of extra calories from proteins and vitamins for growth, sustaining required energy levels and natural skin glow, and for developing resistance against diseases.

3. Dissemination of Information. Disseminate information to adolescents and families on the adverse effects of advertisements in which being 'thin' is glamourized.

4. Inform Mothers about Time Allocation to Food. The mothers should be informed about how important it is to allocate adequate time to the adolescents' food selection and preparation as it affects their eating habits.

5. Inform Adolescents about Nutrition. Inform adolescents on how food at odd hours, going for taste more than nutrition, lack of knowledge of nutritious foods are adversely impacting their health.

6. Regularity of Physical Exercise and Breakfast. It is important to have regular physical exercise and breakfast for healthy living. In fact morning breakfast is essential for the functioning of the brain.

7. **Control Junk Food.** Reduce and control the liking for junk food as it has little nutritive value and harms the digestive system.

8. **Lesser Emphasis on Figure.** Do not become too much focused on the figure. Real beauty lies in having a good figure along with good health.

9. **Do Away Gender Discrimination in Food.** Help arrange information and counseling for families about the ills of gender discrimination as the undernutrition of girls results in their poor body growth, poor eyesight, poor understanding and fatigue.

4

Sexuality in Adolescence

We are all born for love. It is the principle of existence, and its only end.

Oprah Winfrey

Challenge

Sexuality is a critical aspect of development and a challenge to most parents and adolescents. Adolescents have the pressure of learning to cope with unbundling physical and emotional changes, while the adults have to find appropriate ways of checking and monitoring their movements and activities, lest they may take a wrong step. Parents of girls worry even more than the boys and try to explain to them the need of staying on the risk free track. Smita has just turned 14 and has started enjoying sitting close to boys in the class and bus. She enjoys communicating with boys and spending time with them. Smita's parents have become lately quite concerned about her growing interest in communicating with boys and her insistence to permit her to go out with them to movies and malls. They have the dilemma whether to allow her at all and if so what time limits or conditions may be ideally set for her which she will accept and observe truthfully.

The development of sexuality is influenced by the physiological changes occurring during puberty, development of cognitive capabilities and the psychological concerns of the growing up males and females. This shapes the cognitions, attitudes and behaviours for subsequent years. A number of personality factors, such as, intimacy, belongingness, dominance/submissiveness, curiosity and competence, passion and intensity, rebelliousness and negative identity contribute to it. It is as much biological as psychological involving both the body and mind. It determines the extent to which the growing boys and girls experience a sense of comfort in relating to friends of their own sex, and the opposite sex.

All children are socialized to believe from early years what are normal expressed feelings and behaviours of males and females at different ages that are acceptable to parents, teachers, significant others and in the socio-cultural group they belong to. These beliefs are reinforced intensely during adolescence as it happens to be the most vulnerable phase. The role models parents present to their wards and the encouragement they give to participate in different activities shapes their concept of male female relationships at different stages of adolescence. For example, the early adolescents may feel comfortable in mixing within groups of their own sex; the entry in mid-adolescence may signal an irresistible inner pull towards friends of opposite sex; and the late adolescents should show capability to restrain themselves from impulsive indulgence in sexual behaviour.

Low Sexual Awareness

Sexual awareness remains an intriguing and happening aspect of adolescent development as they make a transition from childhood to a healthy sexual adulthood. In most countries, the period of adolescence has become prolonged due to an earlier onset of puberty, delayed achieving of economic independence, marriage and child bearing. It implies that most adolescents are physically ready for sex earlier than before, yet are not prepared emotionally, cognitively and financially to live with the consequences of their behaviour. It is felt that many children enter teenage with little understanding of the sexual behaviour of either own or the opposite sex, with some even indulging in acts portraying them in poor light.

A number of researches suggest that the dreaded diseases like HIV/AIDS begin to take roots in adolescence and assume full form in adult life. Different socializing agencies warn them against getting involved in early sexual activity, lest such acts may do long-term harm to them. This leaves most adolescents open to a range of sexual activities as fun and relationship building exercises, while some may still get carried away towards it, often in contradiction to the adult expectations and/or their socio-cultural norms. Some may fantasize their relationships constantly and push themselves into making of wrong choices and affecting other behaviours. They start to neglect their studies and other activities, defy social norms, resort to disobedience, lying and become targets of rebukes, or get into depression at times.

In Indian society, there are a number of taboos that inhibit the discussion and expression of sexuality in family and public as well. The family tries to exert a good deal of control on the movements and manipulate young people's sexual behaviour as there is a general belief that the youth should be made to abstain from premarital sex. Premarital sex is strongly disapproved both for boys and girls, yet all teens begin to fantasize and experience sexual instincts on reaching puberty due to various influences such as, exposure to movies, cable television, internet, and other media. They get to learn about western images and lifestyles, without the social infrastructure and information about coping with even the most basic facts about their own bodies.

Boys and girls do not become sexually active at the same age. Girls mature earlier than boys, yet the percent of sexually active adolescent boys is found to be higher than girls as they have more opportunities to engage in sexual relations and lesser threat of later consequences, like pregnancy and sexually transmitted diseases. The social permissiveness is also more in case of boys than girls. Premarital sexual relations are however, on the rise and encompass a good proportion of young males.

Sexual Awareness in Girls

Most girls become aware of their sexuality feelings with the onset of puberty, although the body begins to undergo changes much before. The inside development is signaled by the onset of menarche (menstruation).

Nidhi, an 11 years old student of class VI found one day sitting in the class itself that her skirt is stained. She looked at it and felt quite scared and ashamed. She did not know 'what and why' of it. She told it to her friends, some of whom said that they have some knowledge about it. They had heard about something like this happening to their elder sisters, but they do not know what to do in such a situation. They decided to ask the class teacher for help. They went to the class teacher and said 'Ma'm there is some blood on Nidhi's skirt.' As the class teacher was busy correcting note books of students she sent Nidhi to the school medical room. The nurse in the medical room explained to her and the other girls that this is a normal developmental feature that happens to all girls. When it happens they need to use the sanitary napkins. She told Nidhi not to worry about it. The bleeding will be there for 4-5 days and it will happen every month as she is becoming a big girl. Nidhi as well as her friends continued to feel strange though.

The adolescent body also undergoes external changes related to sexuality, which become visible in the growth and mass of body size. During early adolescence the girls' bodies become curvier. There is an increase in body fat, they gain some weight around hips, and their breasts develop. This makes them wonder about rapid growth of body. Varsha, a 12 years old girl of class VI said that she can't even visualize how much she has grown. She wears now clothes 3-4 size larger than three years ago. Her body size has grown in weight by nearly 30% and height by five inches.

Sexual Behaviours of Girls

Some peculiar behaviours of females related to their sexuality are discussed below:

Goofing up. It is an adolescent tendency that surfaces during adolescence. Quite often teens take the issue of sexuality lightly and indulge in goofing up as a matter of entertainment.

Pinky, a 14 years old girl used to go out of her house every evening after telling her parents that she is going to her friend's place. She would go a few meters, meet her boy friend at the corner of the road and go with him on his motorbike to a restaurant. This went on for days together. They went to markets, pubs and gradually became emotionally very close to each other. The physical closeness increased and they got emotionally quite attached to each other. They started looking for more private places to go where they could be more intimate with each other and enjoy.

Pinky discussed her relationship with two of her good friends who listened to every new experience of her with interest. They found a new topic to discuss during their free time, like talk about the exchange of gifts, cards, letters. There was lot of excitement in Pinky as she had never got this type of importance earlier, while for her friends this provided entertainment. Somehow, Pinki's mother got to know of it and stopped her from going out like this. She discussed with her healthier ways of interacting with them.

Interest in Boys. As the girls grow into adolescence they want to know more about sexual development in girls and boys, as well as become friendly with boys. The initial interest may be expressed in the form of glaring at them.

Preeti, a student of class VII was many times caught by her social studies teacher constantly looking at boys in the class and particularly at Mohit. One day while she was teaching the lesson, she could not stop herself from scolding Preeti for not paying any attention to what was being taught. She said 'I have been noticing it for last so many days that these days your attention is only on boys. You are not at all paying attention to studies. You better start paying attention to your work otherwise I shall have to inform your parents.'

The science teacher Mrs. Naidu also noticed Preeti's behaviour. She noticed some other girls too talking about boys in a hushed manner. She heard from other teachers that so and so girl is paired with so and so boy. Mrs. Naidu happened to be a very understanding and observant teacher. She felt that it was the natural behaviour of adolescents. She allowed herself some time to think about what to do without making adolescents conscious of what they were doing. She felt that the adolescents should be given more opportunities to mix and interact with members of opposite sex in a healthy manner. Soon she decided to pick up some science projects in the class in which students would be working in small groups. She intentionally divided the class in a manner that each group would include boys as well as girls. She thought of various activities in which girls would have to work closely with boys. She made pairs of girls and boys for a quiz and mixed small groups to help each other in academic work. She even changed seating arrangements so that boys and girls could sit together. The girls who were congregating with girls but had their attention fixed on boys now got ample opportunity to interact and work with them. Thus their need of attention from opposite sex was satisfied in a healthy manner. Teachers' own attitudes can make students rebel and pay undue attention to the opposite sex. There is no harm if girls gaze at boys or vice versa. At this age there is natural curiosity and attraction towards opposite sex. Talking about opposite sex, looking at them constantly, seeking their attention and pairing particular boy with a particular girl are some of the typical characteristics of early- and mid-adolescent age.

Teenage Pregnancy. In urban areas in particular many of the school administrators and counselors feel that STDs and risky behaviours are on the increase among teens. While parents argue that talking about reproductive health may enhance teens' interest in sexual activities, they together with teachers do not know or feel comfortable about giving the information to their wards. Such reluctance of adults' to explain basic facts to youngsters may result in unwanted pregnancy in some cases.

Renu, a 14 years old girl and student of class IX belonged to an upper middle class family. Her mother had expired 3-4 years back. Except for her father and elder brother there was no other family member living with them. Most of the time after coming back from school, she was alone with a maid in the house. Many times her brother came to spend time in her room and sent away the maid. Her father had changed houses frequently. She had no friends around. She felt all the time very lonely.

One winter evening, Renu complained of severe stomach cramps. To her father's surprise at 1.00 o'clock in the night she delivered a baby with the help of maid in the house itself. Her father was quite shocked. He called the son, but he refused to come and see. All this while, she had been going to the school. Nobody even noticed her pregnancy as she had a lean and thin built. The father called a very close family friend, whose wife happened to be a school counselor. She talked to the girl and her brother at length and discovered that the brother and sister were experimenting with their sexual urges routinely for fun, as both were in their teens with no adult family member around. The brother was 19 years old. The two had ample opportunity to explore as they used to be alone together for long hours. None of them was exactly aware of the consequences, till it happened. Nobody had given them any information about physical and emotional changes during the growing up period. Also there was free access to watching all types of programmes on T.V.

The case reveals Renu did not have mother and father was too busy with his own work. He being a single working parent with responsibility of keeping the house running and children's education could not attend to the developmental needs of his daughter. None of them was prepared to face the consequences. Renu went through deep physical and psychological trauma, as her body and mind were not ready for bearing a baby. There were also social problems when others came to know about the case. She had to carry the emotional burden of the social stigma attached to unwed mothers.

Cases like this occur when the adolescents do not have access to adult guidance, correct information and education on sexuality.

Sexual Awareness in Boys

Like girls, boys developed sexually, internally as well as externally. They enter puberty 2-3 years later than girls. Some of the behaviours related to male sexuality during adolescence are discussed here:

Nocturnal Emission. It is a discharge that signals boys' entry into puberty. Boys have it during sleep. Some boys get quite upset about it if they have not read or heard about it.

Vijay is a student of class X in a co-educational school. He is 15½ years old. One day after the pre-board exams, the students of his class decided to have a party. Girls as well as boys used this opportunity to dress up fancy and unwind themselves after the tiresome examination preparations. Girls dressed up quite attractively. Vijay admired a couple of his female classmates very much. On coming back home, in the night he kept thinking about the party, the girls, and the wonderful time he had had there. He slept thinking about all this. In the morning when he got up he found his pajamas wet. He did not understand what has happened to him. He felt embarrassed and upset but did not talk about it to anyone.

It again happened 2-3 days later. He was even more upset and confused this time. He kept on thinking if there was something gravely wrong with him. He also found that frequently his thoughts kept on going towards girls. He started feeling somewhat ashamed of himself, as he did not want to think of girls at this stage. For quite a few days he did not share his feelings with anybody and had increasing guilt feelings. One day he developed courage to talk to his mother about the problem. He told her that he needs some medical advice, as during sleep he has started passing urine in his clothes. His mother was a doctor and she understood the problem. She explained to him that this was part of the natural changes in his body linked to the growing up process. This happens to all the boys. There is nothing to worry. She told him that as you grow up, the genitals also grow. The testes start producing a substance called semen in large quantity. Like in a glass full of water if you add more water, it flows out, when more semen is produced than the capacity of the organ, with slight movement of the muscles at night due to dreams or movement of the legs, the involuntary muscles squeeze the tissues of testes and the semen flows out. After hearing this from his mother Vijay felt quite relieved and was not worried when it occurred again after a few days.

Masturbation. Masturbation is another common occurrence during adolescence. It is more visible in boys than in girls. It is the act of stimulating own genitals by an adolescent until one reaches a climax (called orgasm) and the sexual tension cools down for some time.

Gaurav, a class XI student was anxiously pacing one day back and forth outside the counsellor's room but did not seem to be enough prepared to get inside. The counselor noticed him and sensed that he has perhaps something to talk. The counselor went out and invited Gaurav to come in. 'Yes Ma'am,' he said and came in somewhat hesitatingly. The counselor after initiating some general conversation asked him if there was something in particular he would like to share with her. He said—'Yes Ma'am, but I feel a bit awkward in telling you about the problem I have as it concerns boys.' The counselor assured Gaurav and said, 'I am here to help you. Please tell me all about your problem. It only makes me happy to help you people.' Gaurav felt very relieved and encouraged to open up. He said that 'In our house, generally after dinner it is study time for me. I go in my room and sit to study, but I cannot study as some strange thoughts start overpowering my mind. I feel ashamed in telling you all this.' The counselor encouraged him to reveal further. Gaurav said 'I feel guilty but I can not stop thinking about girls and then start striking and massaging my genitals ruthlessly. It gives me a pleasant feeling. Ma'am I am not disrespectful to girls. I also realize that I am doing a bad thing but I cannot help. Somehow I feel like doing it over and over and quite frequently I indulge in it whenever I am alone, especially when I sit down to study at night.'

The counsellor explained to Gaurav—'What you are doing is not wrong or unethical? For someone of your age it is quite normal to happen and feel the way you are feeling. Other boys also do it. Even the elderly men do it at times. There is nothing wrong in doing it, if you do not do it too often and at public places. Also it should not be done at the cost of your studies and other work.' The counsellor enquired about his general routine at home. 'What do you do in the evenings? Do you play any games in the evenings?' He said 'No. I either watch T.V. or meet friends at public places.'

The counsellor further explained that at this age hormonal changes are taking place in the body due to which this kind of feeling and acting takes place. If boys play vigorous games or get involved in vigorous exercises it can help in releasing their extra pent up energy and experience less of such feelings. Adolescents can take up jogging, swimming, play football, badminton, cricket or can do any other type of physical activity which tires them out. Gaurav was told that he should not feel guilty about it. Only he has got to be cautious that it is done in private places as we do not urinate in front of people or change in others' presence.

Parents should not scold boys for this kind of indulgence, rather they should explain it and suggest alternative activities to the young boys. Effort should be made to help them rid-off their guilt feeling. In general the fathers are busy with their work and parenting is done by mothers. This task is also left to the mothers but it is better if fathers take the responsibility of explaining it to their sons. This can make the growing adolescent get greater reassurance and feel light headed.

She told parents that all adolescents masturbate to some extent and that they should not punish them for it. Parents should be more understanding and supportive at this age. Some boys who do not perform well in school or are emotionally less secure may derive satisfaction by excessive indulgence in masturbation.

Counsellor's Initiative to Help Adolescents

School counselors, teachers and parents can provide lot of support and comfort to the developing teens. All adolescents need information to cope with the physical and emotional changes taking place in them. It can be given by adults without feeling embarrassed. In the absence of correct information they feel more curious and may get distorted/incorrect information from friends or magazines. Most parents and teachers avoid or are unaware of ways to touch this sensitive issue.

As an example a school counsellor's interactions with adolescents of classes V, VI, VII, and VIII on growing sexuality are reported here. While giving the information consideration has been given to the age and readiness of adolescents. An early adolescent requires the most basic information whereas a late adolescent seeks for more detailed knowledge. A proper climate is built so that they could freely ask questions.

The counsellor began. "When you were a baby, your hands and feet were small. Your height was only 19-21 inches. Similarly your internal organs were very small. Now you have become this tall, your internal organs like heart, lungs, stomach have also become larger in size. When you will be 18-20 years old, you will become full size men/women. The period falling between 10 to 20 years is called transition age between childhood and adulthood. You all have entered now this age range, when you are neither a child nor a big college girl/boy. In a couple of years or so, one day you will become like your mothers/fathers. This period is called teenage or adolescent period. The examples of plants and animals were given. Think of a growing plant. First it is a tiny plant. Then it becomes a bigger plant, it bears flowers, then fruit and then seeds form in the fruit. These seeds are used again to produce new plants. Similarly animals grow up from small to big. When big, they give birth to babies. When we human beings grow big, are mature and get married, we can produce babies. During adolescence many changes take place in our bodies, beginning at the age of 9-10 years. The reproductive organs inside our body begin to grow now. Alongwith the internal changes some external changes set in. Our height starts to increase rapidly and we gain weight. The external changes make the girls look different than boys." She asked the students to enumerate the changes in girls and boys. She found that boys and girls had lot of hesitation initially even in naming their private parts but gradually they opened up.

The counselor continued that "in girls as they grow the body starts becoming shapely. The breasts develop and the hips become round. The waistline narrows. The skin becomes more oily and the face more charming. There is growth of hair under arms and in pubic region. The external genitals enlarge. At the same time the internal sex organs also start becoming active and there are changes in reproductive organs. The menstruation starts in girls." In boys "there is slight change in the facial features. The jaw and nose become larger and the mouth widens. The chin becomes prominent. The larynx grows and at the neck Adams Apple grows. The voice starts cracking and squeaky before it becomes deep. The shoulders become broad and muscles develop in arms and legs. The facial hair and moustache appear. Hair also grows under arms and in pubic region and on the chest and limbs. The sex organs, penis and testes enlarge. Sperm production begins and ejaculation occurs, and there are often night falls. These changes take place 2-3 years later in boys as compared to girls. These changes do not come at the same time in all the girls or all the boys. As we individuals differ from each other, these changes occur early in some and later in other adolescents."

"All changes in the body during adolescence are controlled by central nervous system. It regulates growth by influencing an endocrine gland called Pituitary gland. This is located behind the brain. On receiving signal from the nervous system it secretes a chemical called hormone directly in the blood. There are two type of hormones that start flowing in the body called Estrogen and Progesterone. These cause girl's body to become more feminine and boys body to become more masculine. They also cause internal changes in the reproductive organs. In girls ovaries start developing and in boys testes develop. Development of these glands will make a person capable of reproduction later on."

For junior classes, the differences in the reproductive organs of boys and girls were explained to clarify how these organs remain small in babies and grow fast on reaching puberty and mature by the age of 18-20 years. Both boys and girls were told about male and female reproductive organs as they were curious to know about each others' anatomy. Details of male and female reproductive organs were told to some depending on how prepared were they? The male sex organs are called penis and testes. There are two testicles placed in two compartments of a pouch called Scrotum. Testes produce sperms which are male part of the seed. On attaining puberty under the influence of a hormone called Testosterone, testes produce sperms. The sperms are stored in testes and are carried out through Vas Deferens to penis, which ejaculates them out. The female reproductive organs consist of Ovaries, Fallopian Tubes, Uterus and Vagina. The external genitals are Labia major, Labia minor, Clitoris and Vestibular glands. Ovaries start producing ovum (female part of seed). The process is called ovulation. One ovum comes to Uterus through fallopian tube every month. The Uterus provides seat for it if it gets fertilized by the male sperm (male part of the seed). If it gets fertilized the egg gets implanted in Uterus wall, which supplies food to the fetus to develop. Otherwise the Uterus wall breaks after every 28 days and the blood comes out for 4-5 days. This process is called Menstruation. Menstruation is the periodic shedding of unfertilized egg, blood and mucus which comes out through Vagina. In young girls it marks the onset of puberty. Once a girl starts menstruating she becomes physically capable for conceiving and giving birth. Menstruation or commonly called periods is the normal process of growing up. There should thus be no embarrassment associated with it.

Both boys and girls were curious to know if menstruation happens to girls on attaining puberty, what happens to boys? One girl even asked the counselor—'Ma'am do boys also have menstruation?' The counselor said 'no', because boys do not have a Uterus. The counselor also talked about the issue of menstrual hygiene and when should one see a doctor.

Menstrual Hygiene. Some of the young girls felt embarrassed about sanitary napkins. The whole class was shown the napkin and its packet. Girls were given this in their hands to see and feel it. The initial response was to see it but then they felt embarrassed. They wanted to know how it is used. It was explained to them. They were told about how to maintain hygiene during menstruation:

- Cleanliness should be maintained.
- Genitals should be washed with soap and water every day.

- Sanitary napkin should be changed 3-4 times every day depending on the flow.
- Bath should be taken every day.

When to Consult a Doctor. Some girls may experience discomfort during menstruation which is quite normal, but in the following cases a doctor may be consulted:

- If there is too much pain.
- If there is excessive bleeding and clots are there.
- If period does not occur every month.
- If periods last for more than seven days.
- If there is rash.

Queries of Early Adolescent Girls. The Queries of early adolescent girls were related mainly to menstruation:

Q. 1. Why does it pain during menstruation?

Ans. It pains because of the muscular contractions.

Q. 2. What should be done about the pain?

Ans. A hot water bath relieves the pain. Massage on the stomach, exercise and a walk may be helpful. After lying straight on the back raise the knees up and move them in a circular manner. It releases the pain. In case of unbearable pain, a pain-killer may be taken. Fomentation with hot water bottle is also helpful. Drinking hot drinks gives some comfort.

Q. 3. Can we eat everything during periods?

Ans. Yes, everything can be eaten. It is a myth that one should not eat pickles and sour things.

Q. 4. Is it all right to play and run during menstruation?

Ans. Yes, life should be kept normal.

Q. 5. Is it alright if a boy touches me during menstruation?

Ans. Yes.

Q. 6. We should not do 'Puja' (Prayers) during menstruation.

Ans. We can do everything during this period.

Q. 7. Is this blood dirty?

Ans. No.

Q. 8. We should not do much physical activity during this period.

Ans. We can do all types of work.

Q. 9. Is it O.K. to have periods two times in a month or at times after 2½ months?

Ans. Yes, in the beginning the cycle remains irregular. After 2-3 years of onset it becomes more regular.

Q. 10. I get a whitish discharge.

Ans. It is O.K. to get whitish discharge in between the two cycles, but if it is excessive then doctor should be consulted.

Changes Common In Boys and Girls

Puberty brings in some common changes in boys and girls which are discussed below:

Need of Privacy. The entry into adolescence brings to the fore in most boys and girls the need for privacy. They need their own physical and psychological space in which they can feel free and relaxed without fear or intimidation. As young children they did not like to be in a separate room particularly at night, nor did parents mind their sleeping in their room/bed. The idea is no more comfortable to them. They need a room/place that they can call theirs and in which they may feel physically and psychologically safe and secure.

Niharika is 12 years old and being the only child has always slept in parent's room. She has a separate room but she does not sleep there. One night she heard some noise and when she woke up she saw her parents engaged in sexual intercourse. She kept on lying down in the bed with her face covered and found them in the act for quite some time. Next day again she woke up, and continued to wait for her parents to be doing the same thing. In the morning she got up, but her mind was preoccupied with the thought, what will happen to her when she grows up and gets married. Would she be going through the same painful experience? Off and on she will have headaches and body pain thinking about it. One day she told her mother that she would never get married as she would not like to be in physical relationship with a male. Whenever she heard of a marriage in the family or among friends, this exposure haunted her. She was not able to sleep many nights and felt constantly tired and stressed. Her parents talked to a counselor, who advised the parents to change the sleeping arrangements for them and Niharika. The counselor talked to Niharika a few times and insisted on her to maintain some physical and emotional distance from parents and try to value her independence and privacy as much as of parents. It took a few months for Niharika to get over her separation anxiety and realize the value of privacy in her and parent's lives.

The physical intimacy to the spouse may also be shown in different ways, such as touching, holding hand, appreciating etc. In principle, parents should help the child to learn to sleep in separate room by the age of 5-6 years. Sleeping together is not the best way to inculcate in them the value of affection and caring. Children should be discouraged from sticking physically close to parents from early years also to avoid catching infections from each other and get sick.

Need to Relate to Other Sex. The hormonal changes of adolescence induce in teenagers the feeling of attraction towards the opposite sex. They like to be in the company of opposite sex. In metros a very popular trend has emerged for early friendships between teenage boys and girls. Those studying in coeducation schools and having cells and e-mail facilities remain connected and close to each other. The attraction towards the opposite sex is natural at this age but it has become a status symbol for many. The exposure to TV and other media has emboldened them to express their feelings easily. Schools find it difficult sometime to maintain discipline and keep the classroom environment positively oriented. Some get pushed into it under the influence of peers.

Sonia is a 14 years old girl living in a flat in a Group Housing Cooperative Society. She goes to a private school. In the same building lives a boy named Rishi who is two years older to her and a student of Class X. They both play in the common park of the buildings. Sonia's friends go on coaxing her to acknowledge the extra attention she has begun to get lately from Rishi. As she is cajoled every day by her close friends Sonia has begun to feel attracted to Rishi. Instead of playing she goes and sits with him. She enjoys talking, walking and laughing with him. It is only four months and they are in a relationship. As her friends tell her to be prepared to spend more time with him, have physical touch, kissing etc. she does not seem to be minding it. She has not told anything to her parents but feels she has a steady relationship. She has no idea of the dangers ahead in such baseless relationship.

Those from a traditional family background feel attracted towards the other sex but they either hide their feelings or meet secretly. They feel guilty and do not know how to handle their sexual urges. Sachin, a 12 years old boy of class VI in a government school often wrote 'I Love Mona' on his desk with the chalk. Some other children sitting next to him smiled. Mona felt upset. Another boy Ankit wrote a similar remark 'I Love Kirti' on the last page of his note book. While correcting the note books, the math teacher noticed the remarks.

To some extent teachers and the adults instead of making hue and cry can ignore such remarks. They should however, use these opportunities to explain to students the meaning of friendship and love. 'Love' may be explained as concern and caring for others. Spending time together and sharing similar interests lead to lasting friendships. These also tend to enhance love and understanding between different people. Instead of scolding children they should encourage them to play and do activities together.

In one school, class XI was known to have a very congenial atmosphere for the boys and girls to work, play and do other activities in mixed groups. The teachers and parents had observed this over most of the year, but now it is noted that Arpita and Arjit have got more attracted to each other as compared to others. They sit together in the class and remain together in the games period and free time. They often sit together and talk holding hands. They have developed lot of emotional dependence on each other. They have talked about their friendship to their parents, who considered it to be part of their natural growing up, but gradually their relationship has become more intense. Often Arjit's parents heard that he was taking Arpita on a date. They remained glued to their phones all the time. Their messages became love talks. Their school performance started falling and they refrained from participating in other activities. Arpita would miss cating and be alone in her room lost in her thoughts. She would often cry if parents asked anything, whereas Arjit told his parents that he can not stay without Arpita and would like to marry her after 1-2 years.

The relationship raised concerns. The parents though fairly open minded found the relationship age inappropriate. Both the parents gave their children lot of emotional support and did not blame each other's child. Parents spent time to make them understand that that this is not the age to get married. As the parents and children had good relationship, their talking helped them over time. Arpita's parents spent their weekends with her and encouraged her to make more friends. They made her join a piano class in the evening. Arjit's father started going with him for swimming that diverted his attention and gave them time to be together. Gradually, Arpita and Arjit became focused on their studies.

Such fixations are quite normal in teenagers, and the cases are on increase with parents having nominal communication with their ward. In homes, which are non functional or parents remain out of the house for long hours, have higher likelihood of teenagers depending emotionally on the opposite sex. After coming home children need somebody to share their ups and downs. In the absence of parents they start depending on friends for support resulting in infatuations. At times the emotional dependence may lead to physical closeness, and gradually to engaging in premarital sex. They need to be taught socially permissible ways of interacting with friends of the opposite sex. They should recognize that early relations are transitory. Long-term and steady relationships need investing of many years, standing the storms of time, economic independence, maturity, tolerance and commitment to pleasures and pains.

Vulnerability to Sexual Abuse. Adolescents are quite vulnerable to sexual abuse. In media the stories on sex crime, child abuse, rape, sexual molestation and murder of young males and females heighten their awareness and sensitivity. The feeling is scary to most while those having gone through such harrowing experiences remain traumatized for long time.

Roopali is 14 years old now, but still gets the fidgety feeling as soon as some male relative comes to visit the family. She is particularly scared of persons she can place in the uncle category. One day a cousin of her father was visiting the family. Since mother had to go out, she asked Roopali to serve breakfast to her uncle. Roopali took no time to scream on her mother for asking her to do such a thing. This infuriated her parents. Father just slapped her and asked her not to come out of the room for the day. Roopali locked herself in and did not come out even for food. In the evening the mother asked her to open the door and come out to eat. First thing Roopali asked her mother if the uncle was still around. This triggered a feeling in the mind of mother if something was wrong with Roopali. On assuring that the uncle has gone away, Roopali came out but kept on crying incessantly. After lot of cajoling she revealed to mother that this uncle had acted very nasty with her when she was in class II and was left in his care. In the name of helping her with bath, he kept on touching her private parts and hurting her. When parents returned he behaved as if nothing happened. She kept on telling her mother for a few days that her bottoms hurt but no one took her seriously. This time as soon as Roopali saw the man, her earlier memories came to haunt her. Both parents were very alarmed and decided not to entertain this man again. After knowing this, parents were concerned about Roopali as they had noticed even on earlier occasions her avoidance to interact with adult males. She did not want to be alone in the house at any time. They took the help of a counselor, and watched Roopali's behaviour to help her to grow out of her past experience.

Sexual abuse from relatives and strangers is a reality for many adolescents. It happens more to girls, but can also happen to boys.

Somesh, an 11 years old boy was going home in a school bus after the school. The bus had few more children, in addition to the driver and conductor. After going some distance the driver stopped the bus and handed over the steering wheel to the conductor. The driver called the boy to the front seat and molested him. After reaching home, the boy threw his arms around his mother and began to cry. He vomited a few times, then washed his face and gagged for a few minutes. It was nearly after an hour of crying that Somesh could tell the mother what had happened. The boy was in a state of severe trauma having nightmares and did not want to return to the school ever.

He was taken to a counselor for help. Parents have a special responsibility to protect their children against the evil of sexual abuse as it leaves lasting scars on the young minds and hurts their self-esteem.

Additional Factors Affecting Sexuality

Other contextual factors affecting the sexual awareness and behaviour of adolescents are:

Exposure to Pornography. Most School-going adolescents are now exposed to TV and computers either at home or in a market place from an early age. They can watch erotic movies and pictures that can have detrimental effects on their psychological well-being. During critical periods of childhood, when the child's brain is being programmed for sexual orientation, the mind develops a 'hardwire' for what the person will be aroused by or attracted to. Exposure to healthy sexual norms and attitudes during this period can result in the child developing a healthy sexual orientation. In contrast, the exposure to pornography can lead to sexual deviance, which may get imprinted on the child's 'hard drive' and become a stable feature of his or her sexual orientation.

Sexual identity develops gradually through childhood and adolescence. Children do not have a sexual capacity until puberty but pornography may short-circuit and distort the normal personality development process by feeding misinformation about sexuality. Pornography often introduces children prematurely to sexual sensations that they are developmentally unprepared to contend with. The sexual excitement and its eventual release thus obtained can be mood altering. It has been observed that those who stay away from home and have less parental control are more likely to have exposure to pornography than others.

Adolescents may imitate in real life what they see, read or hear. The exposure to pornography can prompt kids to act out sexually against younger, smaller and more vulnerable children. Experts in the field of childhood sexual abuse report that experience and exposure may be the two possible stimulants of any premature sexual activity in children. Parents of early adolescents may block such sites on TV and other electronic media, whereas for later adolescents they should maintain open communication and discourage them from such exposure. Parents and other adults should encourage their wards to choose healthy means of entertainment.

TV/Print Media. TV and print media are widely used to campaign for precautions against HIV/AIDS, to dispel the associated myths and fears, and the common ways in which it is contracted. The number of persons getting infected is yet on the rise. It is reported that teenagers are the most susceptible group as they are young and adventurous. They get easily excited and have the feeling 'I can do all'. Particularly those not doing well in school and having little family involvement have a higher probability to suffer. They can easily fall in the wrong company and begin to experiment sex with different persons and contract it.

Shailendra is 17 years old and an average student. His father is in business and always busy in making money. Mother is a housewife and not much informed about what to talk to adolescents of the day. He heard several reports of adolescents having sex with girls in nearby colony. One day with a couple of boys he dared to go to a nearby slum where he met a lady, who introduced him to his daughter. He went there again and then kept on visiting other girls in the neighbourhood. He found six months later that he has contracted STD. He went to see the doctor who advised him test for HIV. This made him nervous. He told his mother, who was very upset. He was thrashed by his father. He had to undergo many tests and long-term treatment.

The counselor talked to him many times to restore his courage to live a normal life and think positively. She also recommended that information on HIV/AIDS related issues should be given to all adolescents.

Frequently Asked Questions by Middle and Late Adolescent Girls

The school counselors feel that the early adolescents get satisfied with the basic information given to them but the older ones have specific queries, which they may even be hesitant to ask. The older females (Class VIII onwards) display interest in detailed information about male and female reproductive organs, sexual expression and the act itself, and the girl-boy relationships. Due to their exposure to the media they have some knowledge on these issues but it is not very clear and connected. To a counsellor's surprise in a session on reproductive health, approximately 40% of the girls knew about blue films. The most common questions they asked are listed here:

Q. 1. Why do we feel irritated or depressed before the periods?

Ans. Because of the hormonal changes the girls become temperamental. Also the body gets bloated and some have pimples.

Q. 2. Is it O.K. if a boy touches or kisses a girl during periods?

Ans. Yes.

Q. 3. To what extent we can interact with boys?

Ans. Talking, being friendly, taking interest in each other is O.K. Do not go out with them alone to lonely or private places. It is O.K. to remain in mixed groups.

Q. 4. How does fertilization occur?

Ans. When the sperm interacts with the egg in the uterus, it results in fertilization.

Q. 5. What is a safe period?

Ans. First ten days and last ten days of the cycle are safe. Conception does not occur in general during this period.

Q. 6. What are contraceptives?

Ans. Contraceptives are things used to prevent pregnancy after intercourse. Oral pills can be taken by females and condom can be used by males. However, adolescents should try to maintain abstinence till marriage because of social and health reasons.

Q. 7. What is a condom?

Ans. It is a rubber balloon like thing used over penis by male to prevent semen from meeting the female egg.

Q. 8. Can a girl get pregnant by having intercourse once?

Ans. Yes.

Q. 9. How is the sex of a baby determined?

Ans. The male sperm has X- and Y-chromosomes, whereas the female has only XX chromosomes. If X-chromosome of male meets X-chromosome of female, a baby girl is born but if Y-chromosome of male meets the X-chromosome of female, then a male baby is born. Sex of the body depends on male chromosomes.

Q. 10. How do the sex organs of eunuchs look?

Ans. Their sex organs are not distinct.

Q. 11. Who are lesbians?

Ans. Two females making love with each other are lesbians.

Q. 12. What is homosexuality?

Ans. Homosexuality is sexual act between two males.

Frequently Asked Questions by Boys

Boys need information about maintaining genital hygiene. They should by told to remove the foreskin of penis and clean the white substance collected there. The boys asked mostly the following questions:

Q. 1. Is it alright to masturbate?

Ans. Yes, if it is not done too frequently and in front of others.

Q. 2. Does one become weak after this?

Ans. No.

Q. 3. Is it done only by those boys who are preoccupied with sex?

Ans. No, it may be done by anyone.

Q. 4. Should one feel guilty about masturbation?

Ans. One should not feel guilty about it as it is part of growing up.

Q. 5. Is masturbation done by boys only?

Ans. No, it can be done by girls also.

Q. 6. Does frequent masturbation lead to shrinkage of the penis?

Ans. No.

Q. 7. Does the size of penis relate to male performance?

Ans. No, the average size of erect penis can be between 4 to 8 inches.

Q. 8. Is nocturnal emission O.K.?

Ans. Yes. It is a normal growing up process for adolescent boys.

Sexuality Education

Who should give?

In view of the issues arising out of lack of distorted information, there is definite need to educate pre-adolescents and adolescents about the pubertal changes, while protecting the innocence and purity of the childhood. Be accessible and approachable to make the teen feel welcome. Both in family and school, parents, teachers and counselors should be imparting this information. However, parents are and should be primary educators of sexuality to their children. Some parents and teachers may not be so comfortable because of their personal inhibitions and biases. An honest and open communication with children through childhood, adolescence and young adulthood can lay the foundation for teenagers to mature into sexually healthy adults. Teachers and parents may talk to the adolescents informally and not miss the opportunities when such issues arise. Parents should be able to initiate the discussion on sexuality related issues with their ward while watching T.V. or movies or reading books. In fact, when an adolescent may tell about some event about friends or school, parents should discuss it in detail and help her/him think further. However, the help of school counselors may be taken as they are especially trained to give information on sexuality related issues. School based programmes can be used to provide information and opportunities for skill development using curriculum itself. The mass media can be used to raise general awareness about reproductive health issues.

How to tell and what to tell?

- While giving the information, the cultural background of adolescents and the age should be kept in mind. It should be ensured that the information is not distorted. Adequate time provision should be kept to respond to their queries and follow up should be done. Respecting and maintaining the privacy of the adolescent is necessary.
- Prepare the teens beforehand so that they are able to accept and cope with occurrence of puberty as a normal life event.
- Inform the teen about the what, how and why of sexuality in advance and satisfy the relevant queries by having an honest talk. Tell them how body and sex organs work? Girls should be explained in addition to the changes in their body, the anatomy and the changes in boys at puberty. Similarly, boys should be told about changes in their body and also in the girls. Schools may do well in giving such information in a mixed group of boys and girls.

However, the girls and boys coming from traditional families may be segregated in separate groups, as they may not be able to open up because of their inhibitions and attitudes.

- In addition to providing factual information the discussion should result in better understanding of the developing sexuality among adolescents.
- Along with giving information on physical changes during puberty, emphasis should be given to emotional changes. This will help them to understand their own feelings and body sensations during this period, and to recognize better their attitudes and behaviours towards the opposite sex.
- Help adolescents to develop healthy relationships with the opposite sex. They should be able to develop respect for the opposite sex. Mixing up in groups and doing common activities gives them opportunities for healthy interaction.
- Sexuality education should not be a one time affair. Adequate information should be given at each level of growing up. The issues keep changing with advancement of age.
- Information about contraceptives and the safe period in the menstrual cycle should be given.
- The sex and sexuality are tied up with unwanted pregnancies, dreaded diseases of HIV/AIDS, and STDs. It is in own interest not to have multiple close friendship and indulge in unsafe sex. Compared to adults, adolescents have higher risk of acquiring STD, more so the females due to their cervical physiology.
- Messages of abstinence should be advocated. It works best with adolescents who are not yet sexually active, especially girls. Adolescents practicing abstinence require high degree of motivation, self-control, and strong social support from peers and family. A positive self-esteem, participation in extracurricular activities and academic commitment can be helpful.

- Young people learn about sexuality from many sources, such as, friends, teachers, neighbours, television, books, advertisements and the internet. Parents should supervise the media use, and process what they see in the media and hear from other sources.
- Give support to adolescents to come out of unwanted situations rather than condemning them. We need to convey trust to them that we are there to help them. An open communication with them will be helpful.
- Sexuality education should address in addition to giving information, the issues related to the development of feelings, values, attitudes, and development of skills in communication and decision-making. It should enhance the quality of relationships at different levels. It should help the teenagers in developing in addition to general life skills, skills in negotiation, decision-making, asserting and listening. Adolescents should be enabled to recognize and resist unwanted pressures from other people, deal with prejudices and challenges, and seek help of adults.
- Make the teen aware of situations of sexual exploitation and sexual abuse. It can happen in family, school, neighbourhood etc. One has to be cautious not to land in an unwanted situation. Right from the beginning they have to be taught to take care of themselves and say ‘no’ to unwanted touches to their bodies.
- Help the teen to acquire an understanding of the social prejudices related to different genders and sexual orientations. While the gender differences are socially created it should be acceptable if some boys are attracted towards boys and girls towards girls as they are biologically tuned to do so.
- Parents should motivate their teens to have regular physical workout to be in good physical and mental health. They should encourage them to have some

hobby to spend their spare time pleasantly and constructively.

DOs for Adolescents

- Adolescents are required to do physical exercise and play some sport to release their pent up energy.
- It is good to pursue some hobby.
- They should learn forming healthy relationships with friends of the opposite sex.
- They should try to know the consequences of early sex.
- They need to have parents monitor their activities.
- They should seek information about contraception.
- Believe that sexuality education is desirable for them.
- Inspite of inhibitions, approach adults for information as it will be more correct.

5

Identity in Adolescence

> *You are what you think. You are what you go for. You are what you do.*
>
> Bob Richards

Rimil and Hitesh are students of class XI in a private school. They live in the same area and are good friends. One day when sitting in an area restaurant a resident of the area saw them and asked each one 'Who are you' Each boy told their first name but the person was not satisfied with the answer. On going home the two felt a bit uncomfortable. Hitesh phoned Rimil that why the man behaved in the questionable manner. The two kept thinking about their response. Next day, the two of them decided to ask their class teacher, if they should have answered the question in another way. She asked them to go to the school counselor who told them that the question relates to their identity. Boys pleaded their ignorance and insisted that she explains it to them. She decided to have a meeting with the whole class and explained the issue of identity to them in detail. She said that beginning adolescence, each one of us tries to be independent and different from others. In fact, during adolescence each one sets identity as the goal. It sets in an adolescent awareness of the need of one's personal identity, triggering her/him for its search and engaging in ongoing capacity building efforts to keep the search going. It keeps one involved in activities that may help in finding answers to the following questions:

Who Am I?

This is the first and most important question each adolescent faces. Each one tries to find answers to this question in relation to one's sexuality and social roles, while exploring their world.

Am I Normal?

The adolescents have a need to feel normal more like their peers than their parents. They generally choose peers as referents as they are compatible with them, but they do look for adult approval. The parents may emphasize their uniqueness and monitor peer relationships.

Am I Competent?

The development of the feeling of competence requires that the parents and adults encourage adolescents to identify and test at least one skill on which they are good at and can achieve mastery given the needed opportunity and training. Parents and adults can prompt them by asking questions, instead of telling them what to do. For example, parents and adults can offer ideas about what options others have already tried and found satisfying or dissatisfying (My friend's son Anshu trained in medical biotechnology, got a rewarding job and is very happy about it).

Am I Lovable and Loving?

Adolescents have a strong need to know that the parents and significant others love them. They like parents to set clear standards of discipline and supervision. They need to identify and learn the democratic and helpful ways of resolving the conflicts. An example of evolving identity is cited here:

Shruti is nearly 15 years old and student of class IX. Her brother Siddharth is 2 years older to her and is a student of class XI. They both come from a well placed business family, who see to it that both children get what they need in their daily lives, live well and do well. The family is quite traditional in lifestyle and values and is religious, but does not fuss about kids buying contemporary stuff. Parents have set for Siddharth the goal to go for Engineering degree and then work with the father, and for Shruti to finish college and get married in a good family of parent's choice as she is a girl. Since Siddharth entered class IX he has not been doing well in school. Now in class XI his scores, particularly in Maths and Physics, have fallen significantly. He is not improving despite tuitions. He is quite social and is friendly with a few boys and one girl who live in the neighbourhood. He remains busy learning music and playing cricket. Shruti continues to do well and is in fact always working to improve her rank in the class. She desires to be a well-paid executive in some corporation or a high government official. Shruti has also become very social and has made friends with some girls and boys. She is particularly friendly with one Muslim boy and likes to spend her free time with him. One day when the parents were talking to Shruti and Siddharth about different activities and events in school, they felt that both kids are trying to go on paths different than the ones set by them. They are both doing things differently than parents desired. Siddharth is no more interested in doing well in subjects that will link him to engineering course. They both do not like to do pujas with the family and visit relatives. They like to adopt a modern approach to issues related to their lives. Siddharth has started telling openly that he would not like to do father's business. He would rather prefer to opt for careers in modeling, acting, TV anchor etc. Father felt very offended with Siddharth and communicated his displeasure. He even threatened the withdrawal of privileges of cell phone and TV. This did not discourage Siddharth in any way from doing what he liked. Parents re-emphasized to Shruti the value of being faithful to her religion and marrying a boy parents would choose for her.

After parents had these discussions they observed that the two kids have begun to act quite funny instead of showing any change in their directions. They try to escape the sight of parents. They get up late on weekend and holidays and avoid talking to parents about any issue. Siddharth tries to spend long hours with friends. Shruti likes to spend most of her time in her room (watching TV, phone to friends and studies). Parents feel at times very troubled and have thus approached the school counselor. The school counselor talked to Shruti and Siddharth a few times. She then told the parents that both the kids are behaving quite normal for their age. Shruti is trying hard to find her place beyond the family in school and friends' group. She is also worried about how would she like to be seen by herself and others close to her, and how should others recognize her as a person. Siddharth is seriously exploring what really interests him, what skill he is good at and how can he make an impression on others, inclusive of parents. It is not right for parents to expect them to fit into any set molds. They should recognize that Shruti and Siddharth have different capabilities and interests and they need to be given a chance to explore and develop those. They are likely to do best in areas that will match their inclinations. Shruti wants to be financially independent and is working hard to achieve her goal. This should be seen as her move towards a positive identity than indifference or non-compliance. Parents should in fact give both children a positive environment to nurture their talents and interests and do everything to encourage them to do well in their chosen fields.

The cases of Shruti and Siddharth demonstrate some interesting facts about the identity formation and development during adolescence. Shruti is a mid-adolescent and is confronting the issue of who she is? She has often wondered whether 'I am just a girl, or a Hindu girl, or a student of class IX, or my parent's daughter, or a traditional girl.' She is constantly trying to find out 'Who am I'. She is trying to evolve and shape her personality around the perceptions of 'I'. Siddharth, a late adolescent is less concerned with the question of 'who am I' as he is a boy and is perceived and accepted so by self and others. They both are social and trying to feel assured that they are like their friends loved and given freedom to do what they wish to do. Shruti and Siddharth both love their parents and want to be loved by them.

Another student Shailja is 17 years old. She comes from a conservative family and had an over protected upbringing. Though the parents are very loving they gave her little freedom to grow with. They have had very set ideas and imposed their personal values on her. Right from her childhood Shailja had little freedom to choose things for herself. Be it toys, TV programmes, clothes or food. Her mother would decide every thing. Her parents were fussy eaters themselves and presented only certain foods to her. They chose what game she would play and with whom, what hobbies to pursue etc. They insisted on her being home most of the time. She would thus begin an activity and leave after sometime and say that it did not interest her. She wanted to do with her friends many activities but she did not do lest her parents will not approve of it.

As she grew up into teens, she failed to develop her individuality. She could not say no to anything. She got little opportunity to try out different things. She would ask her parents for everything. Her peers started making fun of her, calling her a baby. In her teens she started to feel angry and guilty that why she can not assert herself. She has no personal identity. When with peers she feels very unsure of her being accepted in the group. Where does she fit in? Does she fit with outgoing friends or with more sober ones or no where? She felt very uncomfortable that she had no inner resources to deal with the situations. She wondered if it was O.K. to talk about boys and other teenage issues like other girls and boys keep on doing. Other students of her age talked about celebrities and imitated their styles. She could not do any of those things. The question—'Who am I?' kept on disturbing her. Though she was loved at home, yet she felt very inadequate and insecure. She was a good student but she does not feel her normal self when with peers.

She has become lately very friendly with two girls who are not good in studies and want her help. They have promised to show Shailja some new things in return, like fashions, parties, going out to places and so on. Not knowing her own mind she started following these two girls and got exposed to things they were in. Shailja felt a sudden change in her thinking and behaviour by the time she came to class XII. She has started manifesting very different behaviour at home and in school. Though at this age all adolescents liked experimenting with their body image, she went over board to see what catches people's eye. She became preoccupied with her own self. Very soon she changed her accent. She told her friends that she preferred being called Shelly instead of Shailja. With some friends she even took liquor thinking it to be an 'in' behaviour.

Gradually Shailja began to rebel against her parents. On every check, she would say 'you don't know' or 'it does not happen like this'. Her parents were abundantly shocked. They wondered what has gone wrong with her as till lately she used to be a very loving child. Why has she begun indulging in wrong activities and was not listening to them anymore. The more they cribbed about her deviating from the family norms, the more aggressive she acted.

The above cases are typical examples of parents either being too strict, or being over protective or imposing their set ideas on their growing adolescents, ignoring the capabilities and interests of the latter. In such situations, the adolescent does not develop an individual identity and does not achieve self- confidence and assertiveness. The cases of Shruti, Siddharth and Shailja bring to the fore many questions the adolescents face during school years related to their identity. The issues revolve around their relationship with parents, friends, and others, values, roles and choices. They are actively searching their own place and role in the family, school and society in a bid to discover 'who they are'? They constantly try out new behaviours and are often not understood by adults around. They are looking for love and positive acceptance of parents and others to feel assured of the qualities they should have to feel normal about their attitude and behaviour.

The identity issue for Shruti, Siddharth and Shailja, like most adolescents, remains in a flux. They have become incrementally aware of the expectations and standards of parents and significant others and how s/he is significant to them. The more consistent treatment they would receive from parents the more sure they would feel of themselves. A major task thus they encounter as an adolescent is of how to define oneself. Is there one set way or more ways to define oneself (the questions cited in all cases)? Some of the changes adolescents experience during puberty bring to them new awareness of self and others' perceptions. They need space to explore themselves and their world. For example, any adolescent like Shruti or Shailja or Siddharth may want to discover for her/himself where s/he can act without taking parents' permission, what place and possessions are actually her/his, the use of which according to his wishes will be acceptable to parents and others. The parents need to be aware of the different needs of adolescents and provide them opportunities to grow into adult roles. They should understand what are their personal, academic and social needs? Adolescents slowly but consistently evaluate and change their perceptions of self in the light of own exposures and experiences, personal assets and liabilities, and the future dreams. They may feel that s/he has become more mature and knowledgeable now (like Shailja). They will develop a sense of themselves with time transcending many changes in their experiences and roles, prior to finding a stable identity and grow into productive adults.

The development of identity among adolescents requires them to acquire the necessary skills and have adequate opportunities, to explore and find answers to specific questions. Parents and adults need to provide safe and secure environments to adolescents to function freely. They require encouragement and acceptance not the criticism. Although the identity related questions surface strongly in adolescence, these are not fully answered during this phase. The questions reappear more than once in a person's life as an adult, but less intensely than during adolescence.

Developmental Tasks of Adolescence

The formation of identity requires the adolescents to accomplish several developmental tasks, which are the indicators of identity and 'normal' development in a culture at that stage. The adolescents need to accomplish the following tasks:

1. New and Mature Relations with Peers. Peer relationships are formed and developed among persons having comparable qualities like, levels of physical, intellectual and social maturity. Adolescents who mature at either a slower or faster rate than others in a group feel out of place and get dropped and have to try to find entry into another peer group of comparable maturity. This process of experimentation is central in identity formation and development. For example Roni did not feel comfortable in the group having Mohit, Sunil, Mita and others as they often picked at one person or the other. In the new group now she can trust Mita and Shalini more. They can freely discuss what they feel about Mohit, Sunil and other boys without having the fear to get into conflicts and pursue their common interest in music.

2. A Gender Specific Social Role. Adolescents develop their own definition of what it means to be a male or female in their perspective. Most adolescents like to conform to the sex roles of their cultural view of male (assertive/submissive and strong/moderate), and female (passive and weak) characteristics. The roles undergo modifications over time. Adults need to provide adolescents the necessary opportunities to test and develop their masculine and feminine social roles. For example, Ronit can tell his father openly what he feels about his sister Sheer and uncle Shan. Sheer can ask her father to not force her to do household work more than he asks Ronit to do it.

3. Accepting One's Physique. All adolescents do not develop and change physically either at the same age or rate. How comfortable adolescents feel in dealing with these changes reflects 'to some extent' a match between their own and the stereotyped definition of the 'perfect' physique for young women and men in their context. Adolescents who do not see their body matching the stereotype may need support of adults around to feel comfortable and have a positive self-image. Sheer may be comforted by her mother that it is O.K. for you to have delayed menstruation than others in her group, and the father can tell Ronit not to get upset by the fringe of hairs on his face appearing earlier than others in his group.

4. Emotional Independence from Parents/Adults. Children derive lot of emotional strength and take pride in internalizing parental values and attitudes. Adolescents need to redefine the sources of their personal strength and move toward self-reliance. The change can be smooth if the adolescent and parents agree on a level of independence to begin with and increase it over time. For example, Ronit and his father may agree that by 8.00 O'clock everyone will be inside home and not go out in late evenings, and increase the time later in small doses of half an hour or so and not beyond 10.00 O'clock. Ronit may identify that his strength is to carry others with him, and can easily live with a given time plan.

5. Making Choices/Decisions. All adolescents confront the task of making choices on a regular basis. Be it entertainment, friends, use of words, activities or career. Each may be asking- Am I able to make my choices? 'Am I correct?' 'Do people value my opinion?' The adolescent's assertiveness, exploring and presenting of new ideas should be respected by adults as this helps in developing maturity. One may be provided the opportunities and left periodically to solve the problems oneself. As a routine the family may involve adolescents in deciding for family vacations, outings, celebrations, purchases etc. This gives them the feeling that their opinion is valued. They may be given some options to choose from and encouraged to make the decision independently.

6. Preparing for Economic Independence Career. The financial independence indicates the achievement of adult status in most societies. Today, this developmental task is not achieved until early adulthood, till an individual completes her/his education and gains some work experience. The task becomes easier if the adolescent has learnt to make realistic choices for study/career to match his/her abilities. Ronit may identify his interest in joining engineering, look at IIT's, Regional Institutes and University Departments, when the coaching will begin, where to go, when are the entrance exams, which institute to apply and what preparations are required. He may also look if he will have another career open with engineering, like management programme or civil services, what jobs will he have access to after completing the programme and what salary will he get.

7. Values and an Ethical System. Adolescents can think abstractly and can argue for and against a perspective and issues with logic and conviction. These changes in thinking reflect that an adolescent has developed to a good extent his or her own set of values and beliefs against which they tend to evaluate their own behaviour as well as of others. Ronit may logically argue whether to support one group of students against the other, what social and environmental issues to take up and why? The adolescents' developing of their ideas and convictions and their acting in accordance with these reflect that they have acquired an ethical system to guide their behaviour, which adults should respect.

8. **Socially Responsible Behaviour.** Adolescents gradually learn to accept social responsibilities as their new social roles give new meaning to themselves and their world now. Their status within the extended group of relatives beyond the family and community is an important achievement for late adolescents. Romil has finished his Board exams and is called to do voluntary work in the community to increase literacy as elders recognize him for his capabilities and commitment. Romil is proud to be associated with the project.

9. **Development of Self-conceptions.** Self-concept is important to identity development. It is the learnt perception of oneself from the present and past experiences within one's physical and social environment. During the process of development a child tends to formulate and reformulate many descriptions of self, such as-I am tall, I am good in studies, I am considered naughty, my parents are very fond of me and so on. These self-conceptions evolve and help in shaping the identity over time. One learns the most fundamental fact about self (what one is or can do) through evaluation and reinforcement of her/his behaviour by the significant others, first the family members, and then the teacher and the friends. Parents, friends, teachers, siblings and others significant in day to day interactions foster the feelings of adequacy, uniqueness, and being special which are crucial to identity. Romil is known as one person who is always ready on call to help the socially disadvantaged in the area.

The cultural context is another important factor in the formation of her/his view of self. Cultures that promote an independent, individualistic self tend to promote and encourage reflections about the self. In collectivistic cultures like India, the interests of the group take precedence over the needs of the individual. This means that to a large extent one's relations to others have defined the 'self' of an adolescent. Romil will be what his relationships with people in the extended family and community will project him. The self-conceptions continue to become more complex as adolescents pass from early adolescence to middle and late adolescence.

Tips for Parents

Parents can act as facilitators in the process of identity development of their wards. Some suggestions are made here:

1. No Comparison. Parents should not compare adolescents with themselves. Keep in view that the physical strength of adolescents is on the increase while adults' strength is on decline. Similarly do not compare the two siblings or praise one at the cost of other. Recognize the uniqueness of each one's different potentials even though it is not in line with the thinking of the adults as in cases of Shruti and Siddharth.

2. Make Home a Safe Base. Parents should make home a secure place where adolescent children, who are exploring life, can come back, feel protected, cared for and taken seriously. Mohit has no choice but to try his hands on different complex activities for his class XII science practical exams. If he fails to do well parents should still be accepting and welcome him at home, and make him feel at ease and talk to him about it. A teenager needs to feel assured that his or her parents will listen to her/him first rather than hastily jump with a judgment, a criticism or routine advice. This would ensure his renewed effort to learn new tasks and remain confident.

3. Agree on Basic Values and Rules. Parents should agree between themselves about the basic values and rules and support each other in putting those in practice. A teenager may not respect parents who are always trying to be at each other's throats and undermining each other. Ronit had no difficulty in conforming to the timing set when both parents refused to negotiate the curfew time of 8.00 p.m., as there is no conflict. A few weeks later however, the father still insisted on 8.00

p.m., but mother said he could be out till 9.00 p.m. Ronit in fact flouted both time limits and came at 10.00 p.m..

4. Set Clear Ground Rules. While adolescents protest you can use sensible rules as the basis for security and agreement. The rules must be:

- Clear so that everybody knows where they stand.
- Set more rules in agreement with the adolescent.
- Consistent to make it possible for everyone to fellow them.
- Enough reasonable to demand support and acceptance.
- Increasingly less restrictive as adolescents become more responsible.
- Do not have rules for everything. While some issues may not be negotiable, there should be room for bargaining on others.

5. Specify Sanctions in Advance. The sanctions, such as grounding or denying of pocket money will only work if they are established in advance and parents have the seriousness to implement them. Rewards for behaving well are equally or probably more important. Rumi will not be able to respect the decision of a sudden cut in his pocket money if parents did not tell beforehand the conditions under which he will lose a part or whole of his pocket money. Rumi expects that parents will appreciate his effort and if possible reward him for good achievement in Board exams. When the father said that he is proud of his son and presented a pen, Rumi felt further motivated, and experienced high self-esteem. Expensive rewards are not recommended.

6. Pick up Battles. A lot of things adolescents do are irritating, but not all are worth an argument. It is paying to praise good decisions or behaviour. Most annoying habits will disappear once parents stop reacting to them. Shamit is disorderly though good at studies. He is not very polite while telling the mother about his school notebooks and party. Shamit's father found many things objectionable in Shamit's behaviour, but chose to pick up his rude behaviour with mother. He told Shamit that he would be watched how he talks to his mother for next two weeks, and if he repeats his rude behaviour he will have to miss 10% of his pocket money this month.

7. **Avoid Corporal (Physical) Punishment.** Practice of physical punishment may encourage the teen to think that physical violence is an acceptable way of solving difficulties/ getting things done. They are thus more likely to grow up and use violence as adults in relation to siblings, friends, spouse and kids. Shraddha slapped hard her younger brother Manik as he did not oblige to bring her water when asked. Manik complained to father who in turn advised Manik to hit back Shraddha. This made both to develop acceptance of tough behaviour and physical hurts/abuse, till they were sent for professional help.

8. **Set Example.** If you do not want your teen to swear, do not swear yourself. If you want them to be kind and generous to other people, be like this yourself. Rumi has always looked at father as his role model. Parents need to be cautious in their behaviour as they are always being watched and imitated.

9. **Do Your Duty.** Do not worry if your teens are not as grateful as you would like them to be? It is great if adolescents appreciate the things you as parent do for them, but do not feel upset if they do not do so. They may not recognize the need of doing it until they have children of their own and realize how demanding it can be. Ronit's parents are always taking care of providing him things best in quality without being asked. Ronit accepts parental efforts but finds nothing extraordinary.

10. **Allow Privacy.** Respect your adolescent's growing need for privacy and give reliable information. Sumit has become increasingly shy as he is growing and desires privacy. He wants his own room and gets angry when someone tries to peep into his notebooks and cupboards. As a parent you should respect his privacy. He needs some personal space to grow emotionally. You should try to boost his confidence and make him understand the importance of talking to parents and trusting friends.

11. Accept and Support Identity Efforts. Trust your adolescent s/he is working hard to establish one's identity separate from parents. S/he needs acceptance and support. Sonu's father works as a director in a corporation and has the identity of an officer. Sonu has an identity as director's son. Sonu is now working hard as a teenager to acquire his personal identity based on some characteristic/achievement of himself. He is doing very well as a student and is known as a good student. He plays cricket, has won some matches and is identified as a good cricketer. The parents should encourage Sonu to keep working hard to maintain and strengthen his identity and help him deal with challenges of growing up.

6

School Achievement

If you can dream it, you can do it.

Walt Disney

School Achievement Is Valued

Abhijeet and his group, students of class X are very happy and excited that they are among the top scorers in maths and physics in their Board exams. So are their parents and teachers. Rohit and Suresh and some others are not happy with their somewhat lower scores. As obvious all of them value high academic achievement, but contrary to the high achievers the low achievers are not appreciated in school or at home. They are made to feel little and demoralized resulting in low self-esteem.

The successful completion of school is considered one of the primary goals as a well as social role expectation for adolescents. The available researches and discussions with students, parents and teachers indicate that school achievement is of central importance in years of passage from primary to entry into middle and senior secondary schools. Good school achievement requires that students have average or above average ability, make necessary effort, have favourable situations to function and have luck. A deficit in anyone of these can make higher school achievement for a student difficult, demanding compensation for one factor from the other. The compensation is however, possible to a limited extent only.

During the years from middle school onwards students experience different types of school work related difficulties. Some feel difficulty in homework and/or in comprehending the different subjects. Some others experience problems in relating with parents, peers and teachers and are thus unable to achieve commensurate to their potential. Teenagers constantly compare and evaluate their physical appearance, intelligence, popularity, styles and school achievement with peers to find out where they stand. If they find themselves in good position it enhances their self-esteem, else their school achievement may be low and they may turn to some ill thought-out behaviour. For not so good school achievers report cards and parent meetings are reminders that they are not being 'good enough.' Low scores threaten them with shame, frustration, helplessness, hopelessness and peer group rejection.

In a school system irrespective of the age the majority of students are of average ability. A much smaller percent is of above average or below average ability. This does not get converted into achievement in a one to one manner. School achievement is a product of the complex interaction of many factors in the personal (ability, aptitude, interests, motivation and personality), home (background, relations between parents) and school (teaching, curriculum, classroom environment, disciplinary practices) domains. Ability and motivation may be general or specific, while aptitude and interests are subject specific and personality factors are broadly overriding. Students who have average or higher ability are likely to be high achievers, given that they have interest and aptitude in chosen subjects, have the personality characteristics congruent to the systemic demands, have favourable study conditions at home, can cope with the expectations of parents and teachers, and are not unduly awed by the prevalent competitive pressures.

Nitin is a student of class XI in a private school in the Science stream with Maths. He has high aptitude for Maths and Science, and has good language skills. He has set Engineering as his goal and has joined a JEE coaching class. He has set for himself a time schedule and does not like to miss his studies any day. Since he joined the school, he has been among the first three students in the class and scored 93% in class X Board exams. His parents and teachers are proud of him and he feels very happy and satisfied with his overall performance.

Schools also have a good number of students who despite their having the requisite capability and effort are not able to perform to match to their potential level. Some of these students may not have the appropriate help available, some may not have right conditions to study and some just do not have the luck. Shirish and Nishit have problems in understanding math in class VII because they did not master the required basic skills at the primary level. Aparna and Ramesh in class IX do not do well in Science, because they did not master the needed skills in middle school. In fact many of them have poor scores either in 2-3 subjects or a very average score in all the subjects. Their low scores imply underachievement.

Many of the students, not achieving high, have in their notebooks teacher comments like incomplete work, brief answers and dull presentation. Their notebooks are generally untidy and handwriting is poor. They do not participate in class discussions. Whenever the teacher asks a question, they avoid answering it as they are often not sure of their response. They look bored in the class and demonstrate little active interest in classroom activities. At times they are careless and not familiar with the proper strategies of learning/memorizing (dates, names, large passages etc.). They also do not do enough practice and revision. Some of the bright students may be as vulnerable to underachieve because of their having personal challenge of some kind, like ADHD.

Facilitators

The school achievement may be facilitated or hampered by one's home, personal, and/or school factors. Some of these are discussed here:

Home Factors

Home Environment. Most parents try to provide a congenial home environment for studies of their children. Some parents however, are unable to do so for various reasons, such as parents having problems between themselves, taking no interest in studies/in academic talks/games/books/magazines and never going out as a family. Some fathers come home late in the evening and do not communicate much with children. Also, some working mothers, on returning home, are unable to help in the studies of children as they are too tired, have other household work to do or are busy with social life.

Relations between Parents. In the family the nature of relationships between parents is a very important factor that sets the tone for feeling comfortable and belonging. It has the power to impact school achievement in the positive as well as negative directions.

Satish 15 years old, scoring high in his class, feels proud of his parents and gives credit of his success to them. 'My mother always helps with my time schedules, taking me to coaching and swimming classes. Some day if she has difficulty then my father happily takes over those tasks. This keeps me assured of my parents being there with me and for me. I am so lucky and chosen.'

Himanshu, a student of class IX has not been doing well in the school for the last three years. He had been a well rated student till class VI, quite capable of doing satisfactory school work in all subjects. His performance started to decline on entry to class VII and became a matter of concern now. His report card is filled with red marks. His father is quite concerned about his lower achievement and met the teachers. Teachers reported that he does not concentrate on work in the school and brings incomplete homework, and that gradually he is moving away from the studies. The father requested the teachers to give him some personal attention. Teachers asked the father in turn to fix regular study timings for Himanshu at home and supervise his work. The father revealed that Himanshu's mother has gone away to her parents and was not staying with him for quite some time. Himanshu being the eldest child has started remaining out of the house for long hours. He keeps on playing in the park with older boys to be able to stay away from unpleasant home environment.

The teacher referred both Himanshu and his father to the school counselor. The counselor talked to Himanshu and made him accept that his performance has fallen, and that no one else but he only can try to improve it. She gave him lot of credit and appreciated his earlier good performance. She encouraged him to get away from the company of the older boys he was playing with. She made him set a new daily routine for work at home, having balance between study and play time. She also asked the father to give sometime and help him in conforming to the routine. He was also asked to come to the counselor after every 3-4 days and report how he was doing, which he did. She tried to reinforce every positive behaviour, which led to further changes.

The counselor advised Himanshu's father to reconcile his differences with his wife as her presence was necessary at home. After a few days, the father brought Himanshu's mother to the school and she was also counseled. It was suggested to her that she should sit with children while they study, do some extra reading and other activities with them, appreciate what they do and show that she loves them. The counselor gave them guidelines on effective parenting. In the next 2-3 months, it was seen that Himanshu's performance improved substantially.

Parents' Time Input. Rahul is a student of class VII. His father is a senior government officer and returns home after 7.00 O'clock. His mother is a clerk in an office and comes home at about 6.00 p.m. On coming home she likes to have tea and then gets busy in checking Rahul's homework. She talks to him about other activities he did during the day, friends he talked to or watched TV etc. Once father is home, they eat dinner and discuss on dinner table their experiences of the day together and laugh and joke. After dinner Rahul watches TV for sometime, does reading and goes to bed. He is fresh in the morning, eats his breakfast and is happy to go to school. His teachers are happy with his progress. When his report card comes he celebrates along with parents.

The case of Chandini a student of class IX is different than Rahul. Although her mother and father both are high executives and have a decent home, Chandini and her sister, after they return from school, watch T.V the whole afternoon and talk on the phone to their friends as there is nobody else there. They barely do their homework and go for dance classes in the evening. Parents on return ask them if they have completed their homework. The answer is always 'yes'. The parents do not have time to check their notebooks or to know their difficulties. Even when they come to the school for P.T.A., they do not have time to follow the suggestions. A quality time input with the adolescent is recommended.

Family Background. The students coming from poor and illiterate families find it difficult to focus on studies as they lack facilitating home environment.

Neetu failed her final exams in class VII. She was student in a Government school in an urban area. The class teacher was frustrated that she was already over-age and has failed again. The teacher reported it to the school counselor and asked her advice. She told the counselor 'She is a big girl and is still in class VII. She has failed several times and has failed again this year. 'Neetu's work has never been complete and is not done with care. She is not regular in school. Her notebooks are very shabby. She copies answers from the books without any understanding." The counselor found out from the records that she was 17 years old, failed twice in class VI and she has failed second time in class VII. She stayed in nearby Jhuggies. On being probed by the counselor Neetu told that her father was a labourer and mother was a domestic worker. She was the eldest of six siblings. Once she goes back from school she has to help her mother with the household work and take care of the younger siblings. She has to cook evening meals as the mother feels tired after coming back from work. Often she has to miss the school when mother goes to the village. Also, her schooling started very late as first they lived in the village. She was nine years old when she was admitted to the school in class II for the first time. Neetu said 'I do not like the class as other girls are much younger. I feel ashamed. Teachers keep scolding. I do not like the studies and don't feel like coming to the school. I have failed so many times that I am ashamed of myself. At home younger siblings make fun of me. Mother has threatened that if I do not pass this year she will get my name struck off the rolls and make me sit at home to do the housework.'

The counselor empathized with her. She felt that Neetu had weak foundation and gets little time to study. As she was over-age and was little interested in studies, it would be better for her to take some vocational training. She was told about various vocational training courses, like tailoring and embroidery, doll making, envelope making, candle and chalk making. Names of some vocational training centers in her area were also told to her. She was also told that alongwith vocational training, she could continue her education through Open school, where after studying for one year she can go to class VIII-Bridge course. No examination is held there for class VIII, and she can then appear directly for class X. This would give her a chance to continue her studies along with learning some skills of her choice. Neetu was not keen to leave the school as here she has the opportunity to meet her friends and to get away from the depressing area she lives in. She was persuaded to take vocational training and go to the NOS centre as she was not gaining anything in the regular school system. This would also meet her need of being with other children, and learning some skill to improve her self-esteem.

Students coming from low socio-economic homes are at a disadvantage in schools and their performance is poor because lack of facilities and stimulation in their environment. There is no one to see their work, help them with studies or to solve difficulties. As parents are uneducated they do not understand the academic needs. For some parents the need to earn to feed the large family is urgent.

Meena and her sister in classes VI and VIII did not have any books and copies till the month of August. When they had to submit their homework notebooks to the subject teachers, they tried to hide behind other students. For classroom studies they would share other students' books.

In metros like Delhi, there is a sizeable chunk of migratory population coming from villages to earn their livelihoods as labour, mason, painter etc. They live in Jhuggis in slum areas. They witness quarrels, alcoholism, and unhealthy adult behaviour. Sometimes children are sent to bigger towns for education and are made to stay with some relative. There is difference between village and town in the quality of education/culture and environment of school and home. In such circumstances the student remains confused, has low self-esteem and fails to achieve.

In contrast, Ranjan is a class VIII student in a private school. His parents are professionals and both have a career. They have been able to enforce good discipline in their life to have breakfast with children prior to their going to school, talk to them about various classes and activities planned for the day, what reading they have done to prepare themselves, ensure adequacy of learning materials at home and in the school, what they read in addition to prescribed books, plan of homework etc. They all join for dinner in the evening and again talk about the interesting and disturbing things during the day. They often critique TV programmes, things on webs and sports. They buy regularly some newspaper and magazines of children's choice. One day a week they all go out and eat somewhere children choose. Ranjan remains excited to find something interesting to talk. It keeps all of them happy and motivated.

Parental Expectations. All parents set some goals for their wards and build expectations around these. If the expectations are realistic most adolescents try and achieve them to a good extent.

Surendra of class X is a bright student. His parents want him to opt for the biology group in class XI. He has done consistently very well in all the term exams and pre-Boards in physics, chemistry and biology. He and the parents are sure that he will score above 90% in his Board exams. Surendra took the Board exam and was successful in meeting the parental expectations as he scored 92.5% marks. This soared the spirits of every one making Surendra extremely happy.

Many students however, find themselves unable to achieve to the expected level, if parents have set very high goals for them ignoring the reality.

Life Events. Certain events in a student's life or the family circumstances adversely affect her/his achievement. For example, the separation of parents may force the student to stay with one parent, resulting in physical, emotional and financial insecurity and confusion in relationships. The death of a family member may require the student to start earning to support the family. Under such circumstances family is not able to meet the needs of the student. It upsets one's routine leading to disruption in studies.

Shashi was a student of class IX when her father passed away. She had two more siblings with little pension her mother would get. She was under pressure to do something to supplement the family income. She started giving tuitions to children in her neighbourhood. She found it hard now to complete her homework. For a couple of months the teachers did not say anything but then thcy all advised her to continue her education through Open School. Shashi did that and kept on earning.

Personal Factors

Effort/Hard Work. Effort is an essential component of achievement. Some students are capable and make the needed effort to achieve and succeed. There are also some students who are capable but are not serious about schoolwork. They either pass at the margin or even fail in some subjects.

Sarika is a student of class X in a public school. Her academic progress has been a cause of concern to teachers and parents for a couple of terms. She either failed in some of the subjects or passed marginally. Her father started getting very panicky as now she is in the Board class. She has not been putting enough effort and time in studies. She was often on the phone making calls to friends or listening to music or sitting in front of the computer chatting with friends. Whenever her father checked her for not studying, she would get irritated and snap back. Her perpetual answer would be 'I know what to do'. Father engaged tutors to give her extra coaching in Science and Hindi, but many times she would waste their time too. Father tried to sit with her after coming back from office at 7.00 O'clock in the evening, but of no avail. Father started becoming impatient. When he started being strict she started running away from the house and often said that she does not want to stay here.

Sarika's father was at loose ends. He feared that she will not pass. As he was anxious, he talked to some of his friends who advised him to take the help of a counselor. He then approached the counselor, who first spent sometime with him to understand the problem. The counselor looked into her previous performance records and noted that she had never done well in studies. In all the classes she was promoted to the next class on some pretext or the other, while she was detained once in class VIII.

Sarika comes from an affluent family. She lost her mother when she was 1-1/2 years old and did not get the maternal care in her formative years. She lived mostly with father, grand mother and maids, and missed the initial stimulations necessary for building the basic skills. Her foundation remained weak and she did not develop proper study habits and attitude towards studies. In school, she was promoted every year on the pretext that detaining her in the class will put further emotional stress on her. To help her meet the class requirements, the father would often do her projects and class assignments, taking out additional information from the internet. This made her dependent on the father. Her academic problems got entangled with other teenage issues. She became very aggressive, showed excessive concern about her physical self, spent lot of time in grooming and trying out various fashions and beauty aids, and developed heightened attraction towards opposite sex. She hardly had any friends and thus a very poor self-image. When counselor started working with her, initially she found Sarika very closed and frigid. She provided her help in building academic, emotional and social skills.

Sarika was very defensive in the beginning to talk about her study behaviour. She kept on saying that she studies for 4-5 hours a day which she was not doing. She admitted that she did not make enough effort and merely pretended about studying in her room. With the help of the counselor she learnt to introspect and examine her behaviour. She was suggested to make a definite time schedule for study at home to complete her school work. Gradually she started spending more time on studies and got better marks in some tests.

The counsellor suggested to Sarika's father to let her give the first term exams at her own effort. Knowing that her foundation was weak, it was suggested to her that to begin with she should leave the difficult portions and first master the easy ones. Guidelines were given to her on effective learning methods, such as making notes of points while reading, underlining the important concepts and words, methods of memorizing etc. Tips were given to her in better time management for her total activities, like time for ringing up friends, playing, TV watching and study related work. Some improvement was seen in the following months, but not as much as needed. She now accepted the proposal of appearing in Board exams through Open School. The counselor called her parents to school to explain to them this alternative strategy.

In schools there are many children who either fail repeatedly in various subjects or stagnate. It happens generally when the foundation is not strong and the present environment is not enough stimulating.

Understanding of Curriculum. Students having above average ability and mastery of the basic skills are quick to understand the curriculum instruction. They know the language, can figure out the context, understand the process of reading texts and formulating answers to the questions asked, and thus achieve high. There are some students who fail to achieve commensurate to their ability in some subject/s.

Abhay, a student of class IX was quite bright. He was fond of Literature, Social Studies and Science. He had a flare for writing essays and poetry. He would often take part in elocution, debate and in classroom discussions. He was fond of sports. He was popular in the class and liked by the teachers. His only problem area was Maths. This was not noticed for quite sometime as he was good in all other subjects and his over all percentage was quite high. But now in class IX, when Maths became more applied, he failed in Maths in the first term exams. The Maths teacher called him and scolded. Abhay said 'Sorry Ma'am. I will try to do better next time.' The teacher calmed down seeing his gentle and polite mannerism, but realized that Abhay definitely needed help. She asked him how much time he was spending on Maths practice. He said almost nil, and often he copied his Maths homework from friends to show that he has completed his work. The teacher asked 'why was he doing this?' Abhay said 'Ma'am, Maths is very boring. I do not feel like doing it. It does not interest me. Thus I try to finish it as quickly as possible'. The teacher asked 'Would you like to improve in Maths since you did not pass?' He said 'Yes Ma'am.'

The teacher told Abhay to set aside a definite time for practicing Maths at home. Mutually they set aside 6.00 to 7.00 p.m. for doing Maths at home. Since he was open to suggestions, some strategies were identified for him. He should practice 6 to 8 sums every day and try to do Maths homework on his own. He should get his difficulties removed every day rather than letting them pile up. He was asked to write all the formulae on a sheet in bold letters and put it on the wall in his room and also at the back of his register. He should learn them every day before starting his Math work. The Maths teacher made it a point to keep track of his work in future. Abhay's parents were made conscious of the fact that he needed more attention in Maths, though he was good in all other subjects.

In the middle school it is compulsory for all students to pursue all the subjects. There are always several students who are weak in one or two subjects but good in others, either due to lack of interest or aptitude in that subject. They need to be made conscious of their weakness and some remedial teaching and practice should be offered to them.

Regularity in Homework. Achievers are in general regular about doing their home assignment. They like to keep their school work updated and if possible move ahead.

Rohit and Anjan both in class X do their homework as soon as they return from school. They then go to coaching classes and try to revise what they did there either before or after dinner, whenever they get time. It makes them feel comfortable and the parents are happy. Another classmate of them Kirti said he finds it difficult to focus on anything after returning from school. He likes to postpone the work to weekend as the teacher may not check before that. He keeps on postponing every day and then he has lot of backlog to make up. This makes him nervous as he approaches exam and then is not able to do well. Every time parents emphasize to him the regularity he tries to find a way of wriggling out.

The cumulative piling up of schoolwork, because of the attitude and lack of motivation (like Kirti), results in backlog. Parents may ensure the regularity in homework, lest it leads to backlog and further avoidance.

Attention Deficit Hyperactive Disorder (ADHD). ADHD is a person's inborn characteristic that hampers one's functioning at school. The underachievement for an ADHD student is a reality. It occurs more in boys and one is unable to focus on the classwork for a longer period. The student is generally restless and disturbs others. He keeps on fiddling with objects and is ready to leave his/her seat on the slightest pretext. The student is emotionally in turmoil and has lot of pent up energy, and has difficulty in following the instructions. Such students even engage at times in dangerous physical activities without thinking of the consequences. They can lose personal belongings easily.

Harpeet, a student of Class VI, came across as a very restless boy showing little concentration on work. His schoolwork was poor. He had bad handwriting. The answers were written in short sentences without giving much thought. Teachers and students had constant complaints against his behaviour. He would push other students, pull their things and cause trouble. When asked about his behaviour he would tell lies and concocted stories. Parents and teachers punished him several times but of no avail. Some teachers recognized his problem. They tried to give him more attention and affection.

Harpreet responded positively to them. It was observed that if he was given a specific responsibility, he tried to fulfill it, though in his own restless and careless manner. He desperately sought for recognition. Gradually the teachers and counselor tried to engage him in activities which would fulfill his need for recognition. He was involved in a project that required vigorous physical activity, in which he really took the lead. The physical education teacher was requested to involve him in manual activities and games.

The counselor advised his mother to help him develop some hobbies- drawing, electronic, carpentry etc., so that his energy gets canalized and his attention span increases. In school he was encouraged to draw. Initially, he traced the drawings, but gradually started drawing on his own. His work was appreciated. He drew a big Spiderman one day by joining several sheets of paper. This was shown to several teachers and displayed in the drawing room for a few days to reinforce his behaviour. He was also helped in improving his academic work. His mother was advised to plan a study schedule for him at home, preferably when there was little disturbance around, and definite play time in the evening. In consultation with him the teacher assigned, to begin with, short intervals of time for each subject and increased the time gradually. To help him in his written work, different subject teachers gave him extra time and help. This also helped him in improving his handwriting. By the time Harpreet came to class VII, his behaviour showed some stability. In class VIII he was made monitor in the class. He was given a chance to play sports and sent for school competitions, where he won prizes.

The significant strategies in case of Harpreet were that (1) some teachers recognized his problem and referred him to the counselor, (2) his physical energy could be canalized by giving him opportunities of physical work and games, (3) he was encouraged to do drawing and electronics to develop ability to sit and do things for somewhat longer intervals, (4) his need for recognition was satisfied by displaying his drawings on bulletin board. These steps resulted in improvement in his behaviour and academic work. Time to time suggestions made to his parents helped them in maintaining a study schedule at home.

Absenteeism. Students may be absent from the class for reasons that are genuine and beyond their control (illness or a serious problem at home, like loss of a dear one). This can happen to any student. Some students try to return to the class quickly and make up for the lost time to catch the pace. Some students however, try to stretch their absence beyond a logical period.

Pooja, a class VI student, had a record of being frequently absent due to her illness. She missed lot of class-room teaching. Her parents though moderately educated did not pay much attention to her studies at home. Parents were in fact overprotective of her as they had lost another child in an accident. Mother worked as a clerk in some office and father had a small business. Pooja used to be under the care of her grandmother most of the time. She was not given any extra coaching at home during her illness. Her grand mother would want her to either sleep or play most of the time. She did not want Pooja to strain herself. If she had the slightest headache or temperature she was not sent to the school. As a result she used to lag behind all the time. She had lot of schoolwork pending. When the teacher explained to her the work in the class, she did not understand much of it. While doing written work she would try to write but didn't know how to do it. She would scribble and make nonsensical sentences. The teachers tried to encourage her to complete the work at home. They would even give other children's copies to her so that she could complete her work. But still her work remained pending. The backlog kept on piling and she could not cope with new teaching. Not feeling well became her perpetual excuse even when she was O.K. She knew that the excuse would work with parents. In school she started sitting at the back seats to hide herself behind other kids so that teachers do not notice her. Many times her parents were called to the school and it was explained to them that Pooja has missed lot of studies and needs to be regular. Change would come in her attendance for a few days then again she would be irregular. The school year ended with Pooja doing quite poorly.

The class teacher referred Pooja to the school counselor, who felt the need of counseling the parents as well. She told that once she has recovered from illness parents should encourage her to do schoolwork. Parents should periodically meet the teachers to find out what was taught in the school during the time Pooja was absent. They may teach her at home with intervals in between so that she does not feel too much pressure. Pooja should be helped to complete the pending work. Other class fellows' help can also be taken.

Parents should make sure that their ward does not use illness as an alibi to avoid school work. There may be some other factors in the environment that may need to be looked in.

School Factors

Workload. The load of work for the student increases beginning middle school. When students reach class VI it is believed that they have mastered the basic skills. They should now be able to read through their detailed course books, find answers to the questions from the lesson and write them independently; master the addition, subtraction, multiplication, division and tables; and learn science and social studies as separate subjects. The student requires greater understanding and comprehension while reading the books. Maths becomes more applied and requires mastery of problem solving skills. In written work the answers become long, and one is expected to have good expression. Students are expected to develop stable and independent study habits.

At the secondary level onwards the courses become even more extensive and detailed. The need of understanding the concepts and application becomes higher. Answers to the questions become longer and descriptive. Questions are asked in indirect and applied form. Frequent class tests are held and learning becomes more result oriented. Once they reach class X, even teachers begin to put pressure on them to function at a certain level because of the Board exam. This needs long hours of self study at home, regular practice and a definite study schedule. They have to balance studies, age related problems, peer pressure, tendency to fantasize, and exposure to media sources. At times student is under too much pressure of studies to get better results. Some students take the increased pressure easily while for some others it becomes a deterrent to natural understanding, interest and curiosity. Making the students study for long hours with no or little time to play can make them disinterested in studies. Also, when a student is not doing well in studies, parents tend to overburden him/her with tuitions, resulting in further decline in performance. At times, students are unable to comprehend what is taught in the class as teachers do not use proper teaching methods. Teachers may need to use appropriate examples, audio visual aids and direct experience to help in better comprehension.

Rohan of class VI was a good average student. His general awareness was good, and his responses intelligent. He took part in most school activities, and was a well behaved and pleasant child. Teachers had higher expectations from him in academic work. As Rohan was not scoring very high, teachers often wondered why he is not able to do well. During PTA meetings, the teachers discussed his performance with his parents. Teachers told the parents that Rohan had the capacity to do much more and perform well if he can be given some extra guidance and coaching. As both the parents were high executives and had demanding jobs, after attending the PTA meeting, they decided to engage a tutor for Rohan to guide him in studies. The tutor would come to the house for two hours from 5.00 to 7.00 O'clock every day. In the afternoon Rohan would do the work the tutor had assigned. By the evening he was so tired that he didn't feel like doing anything more. Parents on their return home would just check 'Rohan have you done your studies?' The reply would be 'yes'. 'Did the tutor come?' Again he will say—'yes Mom.' Parents felt satisfied that Rohan was now putting extra hours in studies. The parents would frequently be engaged at home in their work related discussions. After two months parents were surprised and shocked to find that his performance did not improve. Rather it deteriorated further.

The parents were very disturbed and approached the teacher. The teacher discussed the problem with parents and Rohan. It was found that the tutor was spending two hours a day to help him in the homework. Then he will teach him extra things to be ahead of the class so that when the chapter is taught in the class, he would already know it. He was also giving him work from that portion which Rohan was supposed to do. In Maths too the teacher tried to move Rohan ahead of the class and gave him exercises to do. As a result, neither Rohan mastered his schoolwork nor comprehended the extra teaching. The overload of studies put so much pressure on him that his school performance fell instead of improving.

Many tutors do the mistake of going ahead of school pace, which an average student is not able to cope. Parents should see that the tutor makes their ward do extra practice of whatever is done in the school currently. Also parents were advised to put sometime in the evening to supervise his academic work personally. Sitting with children would motivate them to take interest in academic work. May be one of the parent can take a back seat in his/her career to be able to devote some time to the ward.

Student Teacher Relations. Teaching and learning are based on the simple principle of give and take. It involves a relationship that can be used productively both by the teachers and students. Students who do well usually report good relations with their teachers, which facilitates their learning in many ways. There are also students who do not feel excited about the nature of interactions with their teachers. They always have a feeling of being let down in their efforts to do justice to their potential, as they have not been able to make inroads into the blue eyed group teachers already have created in their minds.

Lata joined this school in class VII. She was consistently rated quite high in her previous school. As she began her class here, she was assigned a backseat. She raised her hand whenever teachers asked a question, but she was not given a chance even if they spotted her hand. Selections have been made for all the activities, and she has not been picked up for anything. She felt very sad and upset about it. Gradually she lost interest in classwork, in friends, and when terminal examination report card came she scored just average. Her lower performance made her upset as well as the parents. Parents decided to meet the class teacher. They brought to the notice of the class teacher that Lata had been chosen to participate in so many activities in her previous school and she even played in interschool basket ball game. This set the chain of changes and in a few months Lata started getting recognition for her work from teachers. This encouraged her to do well and this term she has been put on two teams.

Change of School. Some students have to change their school when either parent gets transferred from one town to another or the student needs higher challenge or s/he is recommended a change as s/he is not doing well in the present school. In any case students need time to adjust to the new environment, standards, texts and teachers. If the students find the teachers, peers and school administration supportive they can adjust easily and maintain their achievement level.

Monika 16 years old passed her secondary school exams from an ordinary school but topped the CBSE list of successful candidates. She planned to look for a higher challenge and thus took admission in the best private school. She was seen by students and teachers as the best student. This reinforced her positive self-image and self-esteem. If the persons in the school environment are unwelcoming and non supportive of a new student the change of school can lower down her/his performance and the self-esteem.

Romil is in class XI in a private school. He has joined the school this year as his father got transferred from Ranchi to Delhi. He did not have any problem in admission as he scored 94.5% in secondary school exams of CBSE. He does not feel the sense of belonging to the school even after three months. He finds the students very unfriendly and ill behaving. Teachers are demanding and very impatient. In the tests Romil's achievement declined significantly. During the parent teacher meeting, the class teacher complained that Romil is not adjusting to the school environment, is not answering any questions, is not making friends and thus his scores fell. The parents may be advised to discuss the issue with the counsellor and try to help him. Romil and his parents met the counsellor and narrated their experience. The counselor heard everything and decided to talk to the class teacher. She told the class teacher that Romil needs understanding and positive acceptance from teachers and peers as he is new to the school. He needs time to adjust. It can help him if the teacher can take some personal interest and sometimes appreciate Romil's work in front of the class to make him feel comfortable. In the next test, when Romil got highest marks, she announced it in the class. This set the change in his self-image as well as in the relationships with other students.

Other Distractions

Some other distractions in the environment (family and outside) that may make many students to develop poor concentration may be their high indulgence in outdoor activities, movies, TV watching, hanging around with friends in restaurants, partying etc. While the focused students may still succeed in concentrating on their schedule of work, the others may develop a casual attitude to academic goals and overtime lag behind.

Manil of class XI has his goal to get through pre-medical tests. He does not miss his coaching class any day, nor does he like to deviate from the schedule of work set for home. He watches TV at the dinner time only and avoids talking on phone while studying.

Ishan is 15 years old studying in class VIII in a good public school. His parents have a reasonably good and financially sound background. They are both highly educated professionals, very social and ambitious. Once Ishan entered the secondary school he developed liking for luxury items in electronics, fancy bikes etc. He also became very social going to the parties of elite and big business family kids. He would go partying with them all evening, see movies and go to clubs. He started getting disenchanted with doing homework or going for study classes. He would frequently miss school on one pretext or the other or go and leave school with friends and come home late. Parents were busy in their life and came to know of it only when he failed in class VIII. He had not worked hard in past two years and has lost confidence in his ability to cope. As the luck would have it, he failed for the second year too. Parents are finally talking to a counselor in addition to the school counselor.

Pressures and Stress

The pressure on students to achieve high in schoolwork may emanate from various sources (the contents of activity, peers, teachers, parents, context of achievement) and may affect performance positively as well as negatively, depending on the predispositions of students.

Contents of Activity. Most schoolwork is time bound. An activity is required to be completed within a certain time, memorized and evaluated using a preset standard. Speed and power are thus inherent in schoolwork and constitute pressure.

Onkar and Shivam both are classmates in class VII. Onkar is sharp and good in writing. He finishes his test papers in time and revises. Shivam is bright and focused. His writing is good but uses long expressions. He writes a lot for every question during tests and often has difficulty in completing the paper, and then gets nervous. Shivam always achieves lower than Onkar. Shivam is advised to do more practice and be concise in writing to finish the work within the set time limit.

Peers. Some student/s may gain in the company of peers and some may lose depending on the nature of influence. To be or not to be like others in the peer group is a dilemma most adolescents face. There is a strong urge to be like peers, behave like them, go to same places, and participate in same activities. The need to fit in the group can bring in the student either positive or negative changes.

Neel, 15 year old and got into a peer group at the school, who would go out during school and not return to classes. Gradually, they started losing track of the work done in the class. When they had the tests they had lot of pressure to perform. Neel started having regular headaches and could not do well.

Adolescence is a very impressionable stage. They like to be with friends for long periods, and influence each others' thinking, mannerism, ways of dressing up without realizing the harm they are doing to themselves

Pressure of Competition. Parents desire their wards to do their best in school. To this end they invest substantial resources and repeatedly put pressure for joining coaching classes, study late and not waste time in meeting friends. As the exams come nearer they lose sleep, get stressed and transfer their stress to their wards. Many students find senior classes highly competitive and stressful as they are also aware of the tough competition for getting into a good course/college. The thought of preparing for the next test, coping with the vast course before the Board exams, the pressure from teachers and parents to achieve high and high social expectations put lot of pressure on them. The thought of Board and entry exams becomes frightening. The stress at times clogs their minds and they are not able to study.

Mrinal is a very good student going to take his Board exams for class XII this year. He has been told since he was in class VII, that his goal should be IIT. He is put into coaching classes since class IX. He has taken so far all the tests and exercises of coaching class. He is putting all his time in studies, not going out with friends or family or for playing. In the month of January he began to feel very exhausted, disinterested in studies and lost appetite. He is getting worried about the demands of work for Board exams and IIT JEE. As and when parents remind him of exams he develops headache and gets irritated. In early February one day, he just threw up and felt incapacitated by severe body pain. A medical examination was done but nothing was found that could be the cause. He was then advised to see a counselor, who suggested to him to take a break for a week and stop thinking about exams. He was taught some relaxation exercises. Parents were also asked not to put any pressure as it puts him under lot of stress. After having the break, Mrinal felt refreshed and did extremely well in his exams.

Rita is also a classmate of Mrinal and is taking class XII Board exams and pre-medical tests. Her parents are both physicians. She eats nutritious food and goes out with them on regular walks. She studies according to her schedule and goes for coaching. At dinner time and while getting ready for school she talks to her parents about various issues and difficult portions she has. They encourage her to read those things twice and write. Parents also assured her that it will be O.K. with them even if she does not get into medicine. She can do so many other things. She did extremely well in her class XII and got into a good medical college.

Stress can thus lead to higher as well as lower achievement. Stress can be due to too much homework and rigid schedule of studies, or doing many activities at the same time, such as dancing, music, sports, computer etc. It is important for adolescents that they eat nutritious and balanced diet and stay away from stressed persons around exam time. Stress is contagious and can get to others. One should learn to look positively at future, and think of different activities and topics and relax. The chilling out is important. As most students study for long hours they should not ignore eye care. They should try to sleep well to be able to feel fresh in the morning.

Summing Up

Diversity characterizes achievers as well as underachievers. There are wide intra group differences among both. They have different capabilities and situations of functioning that can result in good or lower performance. Most cases reflect that neither achievement nor underachievement originate wholly in home, personal and school domains. For most adolescents in schools, it may be a cumulative manifestation of the various facilities or difficulties experienced in different areas of life.

In middle school onwards students have to deal with personal needs, growing up issues, higher academic demands, more complex school structure and declining parental involvement. Those who adjust to these continue to achieve well, while those unable to adjust begin to achieve low. Schools have to do their share of work but they can not succeed without increased home support. While the parents of achievers are happy to contribute to the success of their ward on a stable basis, the parents of underachievers face various problems like seen in many cases above. Many of them put the blame on the adolescents that they like independence and little family involvement. Students though felt that they can do better with parental involvement and positive appreciation of their schoolwork. Parents of such students thus need to be encouraged to (a) have open communication with their teens; (b) enforce rules in a way that adolescents may learn to value independence along with responsibility; (c) not impose their aspirations on their wards, and (d) show the importance and value of education for themselves and their wards by encouraging the habit of regular homework and self-study.

The scenario for all students seems to be quite complex against the expectations set for them in this millennium. It is more so for low and underachievers. As they proceed through school years they are expected to learn to analyze, synthesize, and evaluate information; be able to effectively communicate with others; achieve proficiency in different subjects; develop ability to work with different groups; be self-motivated and responsible for their decisions and actions; and have commitment to their families, peers and communities. The low and underachievers may fall short on more than one of these dimensions, and remain deprived of the positive outcomes of education in society (employment opportunities, higher earnings, participation in the technical and demanding occupations of the future), and higher self-esteem. They may need help.

School Help. Some schools take positive steps to help students improve their achievement through counselling. One such example is reported here:

In a school, during the month of August after class XII students of Humanities stream completed two months of the term, the teachers informed the counselor that the girls (majority in the class) were not serious about studies. They were not learning their lessons, not completing their work and also not doing any self-studies at home. Teachers felt that despite their constant reminder students showed no change.

The economics teacher asked the school counselor to motivate them as it was a Board class and their result was going to be poor. The counselor consulted other teachers who had the same opinion. Most of these students have become careless now, though they were O.K. till class XI. The class teacher said that most of the time the girls talked about boys, friendships and meetings outside the school. They were also confused about various teenage issues and did not concentrate on studies.

When the counselor talked to the students some of them said that the teachers were unhappy, but they do study. When asked if they devoted enough time to studies at home, they all said 'yes'. They reported 'their homework takes lot of time. The completing of Home Science practical file takes whole afternoon leaving little time for other subjects. Home Science requires collecting lot of material from magazines, cutting and pasting.' On further probe they said they sleep in the afternoon and while away their time. They sit down to study only in the evening after 6.00 O'clock. First they do the Home Science file which takes long time. What they thought as 'self-studies' was only finishing homework. They showed little seriousness for schoolwork as they were not interested in a career.

To bring a change, the counselor gave tips on time management and a study schedule to follow. They should put two hours (3.00 to 5.00 o'clock) in homework and in the evening devote sufficient time to self-studies. They should keep a time slot for each subject and do Home Science file in the end as it carried only 5 marks. Various career options were discussed in the group to motivate them for some careers. Extensive career information was given on job oriented courses in polytechnic and other vocational institutes.

The counselor took note of various teenage problems that have become a major source of distraction for them. The discussion was held on issues related to physical and emotional changes during adolescence and attraction towards opposite sex. It was noticed that many of them did not discuss these issues with parents as many came from traditional families and felt hesitant. Teachers also snubbed them often. The guidance period provided an open forum to them to discuss these issues.

Another time the low achievers were helped through organized small discussion groups. One such case is cited here:

A group of seven students of class VIII (having very low marks in class VII and in the first term exams) were selected for group counseling to help them to improve their classwork. Teachers reported that these students took little interest in studies. They were given group counseling for 8 sessions between 1st and 2nd term exams during the games and library periods. Some improvement was seen in their 2nd term exams, and a marked difference in the 3rd term exams results.

In the first session the counselor focused on developing a warm and understanding relationship with students and assured them of confidentiality. In the subsequent sessions, the counselor enquired about how they study, what they think of themselves and what others think of them. They opened up after some reservations. They revealed 'We are not good students', 'can not do well', 'have no liking for studies', 'are not liked by teachers'. 'Teachers start scolding us from the moment they begin, parents think low of us as if we can not do anything', 'peers and siblings think we are useless', 'school environment is not good', 'teachers do not teach properly and miss the classes', 'they do not remove our difficulties and scold us', 'we do not like the class environment'.

The counselor thus helped them in exploring their feelings and in analyzing their study behaviour. They set short-term goals for themselves and started working on them. The counselor reinforced them every time they reported a positive step. From short-term goals they were led to set long-term academic goals. In the end students became more objective. They were able to understand and analyze their study behaviour. Their following statements indicated these gains:

> 'Now I can answer more questions in the class as compared to earlier. Teachers regard me better and treat me like other students. Now my parents think that our daughter has abilities and can be a good student if she puts in some more effort. Earlier if my friends talked

about studies, I used to detest as I could not do that much. Now when they come, I also talk about studies. I like it now. Earlier, when I did not know something I hated studies, but now I try reading it carefully. Now I do my studies daily. Earlier I never used to ask anybody if I did not understand but now I ask. I did not know that studies need regularity. Now I am able to find time for play and studies. I have become better in Maths and History. I read four subjects a day, as compared to one or two earlier. Now I am able to understand greater portion of the course.' They were also able to identify more weaknesses.

Do's for Teachers

Some of the do things for teachers to help underachieving students may be:

1. Be Sensitive and Tolerant. The teachers have to be sensitive to the needs of bright students so that they can maintain their level of effort and morale. They have to be even more sensitive to the needs of low/under achieving students. Teachers are their role models in the school. The classroom teaching should relate to the level of understanding of the student and satisfy their curiosity. All students need to be encouraged and those doing poorly should be given more encouragement than punishment and condemnation. The practice of putting them to shame and making negative remarks does not improve a student's performance. It makes the person feel that 'I am not good,' 'I am not a capable student'. It further alienates them. Effort should be made to gradually pull up students by strengthening their weaker areas along with the strong ones.

2. Listen to Student. The teacher should give an ear to what the student has to say either for wanting to know more or for not doing the work properly. Opportunity should be given to all students to ask questions in the class and to express themselves.

3. Understand the Background of Student. Understanding the background of a student will help in identifying an appropriate strategy for her/him. A low achieving student coming from an underprivileged home may require more help in the school, whereas students from educated families may be given references of appropriate sources. Special events in a student's life may be given appropriate consideration and expectations adjusted.

4. Accept Individual Differences. The high as well as low achievement in two students may be due to different causes and thus the two cases may require different handling.

5. Create Positive Atmosphere. Create an atmosphere of love and understanding to encourage all students. To this end recognize their small achievements by making positive remarks and showing their work to others in the class. Make each one feel important by giving opportunities to participate in various activities and small responsibilities (collecting copies, be responsible for decoration, mind a particular row etc).

6. Guide Parents. Meet the parents of underachievers more frequently than others and give them guidelines about what students should do to learn and memorize. Definite tips may be given on setting aside time to study and work on weak areas (practice tables in Maths, reading of books, finding answers from books on their own, learn spellings etc). The household work should be distributed among all children (male and female). Parents should also be advised to take their wards to parks and historical places to give them different experiences. Guide parents of good students for location of helpful materials.

7. Adopt Effective Teaching Methods. Some teachers are very effective in teaching the contents as it raises students' excitement, curiosity and imagination. They use diverse teaching methods, such as audiovisual aids, examples, opportunities to explore and give direct experience of the objects and places to connect the contents of syllabus with the varied levels of understanding students display.

8. Change Seating Arrangement. Make the low achievers sit with good students to motivate them. Use peer helpers. Make groups of students, like having 2 good, 2 average, and 2 low achievers. It may help the low achievers and also encourage the good students to develop their skills further.

9. Time Management and Home Study Schedule. Teachers should inculcate effective study habits in students. Guidelines may be given to them about how to manage their time for various subjects, and how to set and follow a home schedule.

10. De-Stress Students. Free students from undue pressure. Many tests, loads of homework, scolding and pressure for extra study cause anxiety.

11. Adopt a Pleasant Stance. Adopt an approachable stance to motivate students for learning. Students feel comfortable with helpful, friendly and firm teachers in getting their difficulties solved, whereas with a strict teacher they start ignoring the studies.

12. Take Help of School Counselor. Take school counselor's help as they can better appreciate the needs of learners, causes of underachievement, methods of motivating and can help students change their behaviour in a positive direction.

13. Emphasize Regularity and Hard Work. The regularity and hard work are keys to good performance, though a thorough knowledge of basic concepts is essential. Among the students referred to the counselors for low achievement, it is seen that most do not have a consistent study schedule at home, a fixed study place, good study methods and the emotional support of parents. Some study while the T.V is on and others do not spend enough time on reading the books and do not practice writing.

14. Inform about NOS. Repeatedly failing and stagnating students of classes VII, VIII, IX and higher may be advised to continue their education through National Open School as it provides to them wider choice of subjects and five opportunities to clear a paper. A student can opt to do two-three papers at a time. On failing in one subject one does not have to repeat all the five subjects.

15. Advise Sports. Advise adolescents to participate in sports regularly to canalize their physical energy.

Tips for Parents

1. **Give One Clear Message.** Parents should agree between them to give to their ward one clear and positive message about expectations from them in schoolwork. Their positive talk to each other about the student within his or her hearing may be more effective and can dramatically change her/his behaviour and self-perceptions.

2. **Maintain Study Schedule.** Parents should see that their wards follow some study schedule at home. Whatever they learn in school, they should revise at home and do some general reading related to specific subjects.

3. **Model Behaviour.** Parents may model certain behaviours. If adults talk about the boss in a negative light or express such views (punctuality is not required, work is boring and dissatisfying), their ward gets the message that hard work and regularity are of no value. They need to learn the value of regularity and consistency in studies.

4. **Make Them Work.** Let your ward do the schoolwork independently. Struggle is necessary to the development of self-confidence. There may be times when your adolescent is frustrated by a difficult task but resist the temptation to solve the problem for her/him. Your ward will learn and grow from this experience to gain confidence to face the next challenging task.

5. **Fixed Study Place.** The child should have a fixed place for study at home where all study material can be kept. The place should be free of disturbance.

6. **Positive Approach.** Appreciate whatever your ward achieves and encourage to do better by demonstrating your trust in her/him. Do not overreact to her/his success and failure, because it can put either intense pressure to succeed or despair in dealing with failure.

7. **Encourage Appropriate Learning Methods.** While learning very long materials first make them learn it in parts and then study the whole. Encourage meaningful learning. Emphasize to underline the keywords, keeping points in a

summary form and making tables and charts. In the end, recapitulation of the material learnt and repeated practice can be very helpful in memorizing. On the night before a test, make your ward review materials before bedtime as it would help in the retention of studied material.

8. **Monitor Use of Electronic Gadgets.** Recognize that media (TV, Videos, internets, and cell phones) along with many good things convey wrong messages to growing teens, which confuse them. The types of clothing, mode of leisure, types of relationships shown lead them to fantasize and move away from studies. Many teens complain that when they sit to study they can not concentrate after so much excitement.

9. **Competition Necessary.** Recognize that competing is necessary for students to achieve with self-confidence, although excessive competition is harmful.

10. **Avoid Over-scheduling.** Do not schedule your ward too much. Make time for some extra-curricular activities, rest and sleep. Encourage healthy sleep patterns.

11. **Value Nutritious Food.** Be sure your ward starts the day with breakfast and has three regular meals.

12. **Set Realistic Expectations.** Have realistic expectations. If his/her abilities are slightly above average, encourage but don't expect her/him to be at the top of the class. To that end give her/him support, have faith and find ways and opportunities of demonstrating it to them.

7

Net Technology

Capability is not as important as connectivity.

W.T.G. Richardson

Mr. Prasad has bought a cell phone and is trying to figure out how to perform various functions on it. He is experiencing difficulty in operating it, but to his surprise his nine years old son fiddled with it and demonstrated how to use many of the functions. Another friend Mrs. Wadhwa has acquired a laptop a few days ago and is learning how to use it for managing her accounts, but her 13 years old daughter can already use its many functions. Similar situation prevails in many homes with youngsters being quite at ease in using technological gadgets and grown ups taking time to feel comfortable. Most of these gadgets use net technology and are designed for multiple functions of information, communication and entertainment (Convergence).

Technology Challenge

Adolescents are great fans of technology as it touches their lives in multiple ways. Technology has crossed all frontiers and brought together persons of different cultures, languages, geographical locations, levels of social hierarchy and ages, and people are using it for keeping themselves informed, to communicate, and entertain. Day, time, place are no more the constraints to what they wish to do. They use computers (Internets and Webs), I-Pods, Cell phones, cable TV to explore and reach the earlier uncharted, unrecognized and invincible territories and accomplish from simple to the most complicated tasks. A school adolescent in Delhi is able to play a challenging game of wit and intellect on computer with a student in Seoul, another in London and one in California as a team and connect to find solutions to complex problems. They are able to engage collectively in problems of common interest without coming face to face, and yet experience success and satisfaction. The reach power of new technology is tremendous but it also has a darker side, making it necessary for all users to use it with a human face and caution.

Internet and Web. Adolescents use the internet and webs on a regular basis as they are the most computer savvy groups. They have strong urge to stay informed, connected, and in control of their situation. They use the internet to gather information for their various projects, check out sport developments and scores, and practice their social skills. Whenever they are struck by a problem or need more information on a subject they just access the web. Search engines such as Google and Yahoo provide access to vast information. Most of them feel very disappointed and helpless when they fail to access the net even for a few minutes. One of the byproducts of using internet and webs is that the new generation (Gen-X) has become quite individualistic and independent. They can find persons on the web sites to share their views, which they may not be able to discuss with their parents and teachers. A good per cent are even carried away by the misconstrued notion that reading books is no more necessary as the information on the net would be authentic and complete. The use of internet is helping to save many human hours, money, and energy, and pushes one to move faster to be at the forefront. It is central to the life of all age groups. The access to cyber technology has enhanced their personal power, skill range, choices, and self-esteem.

E-mail. It is used by most of the educated persons inclusive of adolescents for sending messages across the world to exchange photographs and videos, and to store and retrieve these. They can forward quizzes or interesting facts, jokes etc. to a large number at the same time. Many of the adolescents now have personal e-mail IDs to communicate with their peers.

They can maintain their privacy as one needs the password to open the account. It is very elating for the teenagers but it is at times, disturbing for the parents as they have no clue with whom their wards are in contact.

Net In Classroom Instruction

A large number of school going adolescents in India, particularly in metros and big cities, are exposed to the available cyber technologies and are using these to enjoy the multiple advantages. They are familiar with e-bay, Google, Yahoo, etc. These developments have been challenging the teachers to change the conventional models of teaching. They are trying to make constructive use of the computers for designing and transmitting the instruction to students in an interactive manner. This makes learning interesting to students and enriches their subject knowledge.

Mrs. Subramanium, a progressive class IX history teacher, while teaching a chapter, encouraged children to seek more information from the internet. She gave reference of some sites related to the topic and asked them to locate more addresses and information at their own. Before finishing her class she said "let us see who is able to bring more information on this topic tomorrow." On coming home students were quite excited to explore the net for compiling the related information. Next day, Mrs. Subramanium found that students have brought a big pool of information on the topic. All were excited to share the different pieces of information they had collected. Some students read and showed pictures from the print outs they had brought whereas others shared the main points they had jotted down from the net. In the end, Mrs. Subramanium noted on the blackboard the new points that emerged from the discussion, which the students also noted. She confessed that 'with you guys even I am learning new things on the topic.'

Similar to Mrs. Subramanium many other teachers are encouraging students to explore more and more information on the net and thus take teaching beyond the limits of the prescribed text books. Students are getting motivated to develop the habit of searching the web for information while sitting in the comfort of own house. Some older teachers, who are not so computer savvy, may be at a disadvantage, yet they can make their students benefit by encouraging them to research on the net and appreciate the work they undertake.

In another school, the science teacher of Class XI assigned to the students a science project as homework during summer vacations. Nithish a boy, skilled in the use of computers and a conscientious student, decided to prepare his project on a novel topic. He searched the net extensively for the relevant and recent information, and supplemented it with information from the books. He studied those intensively, made selection and drew his own interpretations. He made plan for a power point presentation using the computer. He also morphed the selected pictures and created sound effects for the narrations. He put the whole project on a CD and brought it to the class. He requested the teacher to permit him to present his CD on the projector for which the arrangement was made. The teacher and the classmates highly applauded Nitish's presentation of the project. It was followed by a question answer session, which he thoroughly enjoyed and answered while the teacher kept on adding more details. Other students also used net to enrich their answers.

Other Uses and Concerns

The net technology is useful in all fields at different levels, beginning from getting information on recent researches to its use in every day operations like ticketing, banking, medicine, accounts, media, tourism, data processing and in designing. It can offer multiple job opportunities to adolescents. They should thus be helped to advance their skills in the use of computers by training on different programmes they may choose.

Most adolescents are ahead of their parents and educators in computer skills and they tend to misuse it at times. With a click of button they can change the contents they are reading without letting anybody know what they were accessing. Thus adolescents get access to lot of unwanted information without the knowledge of their parents. They require careful monitoring of contents they explore and the amount of time spent on the computer as they get easily swayed to go over board in its use. Parents should therefore allot to their ward specific time for computer use and encourage time management. The use of internet should not be promoted at the cost of neglecting other activities necessary for their age. Even in the families not having a computer at home, the adolescents use computers in schools, market places, cyber centres to access internet. In fact, the day is not far when all schooled children and teens would have become active participants in cyber space. This pushes to the fore the need for the parents to guard their wards against the possible misuse of these technologies and its adverse effects on them.

Problem of Early Exposure

Many parents encourage their offspring from an early age to use computers and the internet ignoring the darker side of the technology.

Aditya, a 10½ years old boy has been using computer for last 7 years. His father works for a computer firm and has always been talking of advancements in technology and the rewards one can enjoy being computer savvy. By now Aditya has mastered the basic computer skills and has demonstrated the mastery of some complicated computer programmes, like Adobe Photoshop, Adobe Flash and Dream Weaver. He has learnt how to access different websites for information, use and modify popular programmes and play games. He has been given on this birthday his own computer and it is placed in his room. Aditya is bright, reasonably social and tries to interact with his friends and most guests visiting the family. Most evenings he spends with friends, either at some friends' house or at his own house. Recently it is noticed that they do not play outside or in the common area in the house, but as soon as they are together they rush to their rooms and stay there the whole evening. They are always busy playing different computer games and have got interested lately in war games. Aditya's mother comes into his room off and on to pass on snacks. One day Aditya's mother noticed that when she tried to stay in the room a little longer, they began doing an unusual hush hush with suspicious smiles on their faces. She got a little concerned. Next day, when these children came and went with

Aditya to his room they closed the door behind them. The mother asked them to come downstairs for snacks and without giving them any notice she went into Aditya's room. She was aghast to see that they had accessed a pornographic site.

Without making much noise about it, she told Aditya that she feels very lonely and it would be good to keep the computer in the lobby so that she can talk to him while doing her work in the kitchen, and he and his friends can be on the computer. She requested the father to block the pornographic sites on internet without talking about it. She also talked to the parents of other kids to do the same. She made a point that they should play outdoor games for sometime in the evening as it would put their energy to good use and make them feel fresh. The computer games were now regularly monitored. Aditya's parents felt that if he continued to have unrestricted access to computer, TV/videos, he may develop over the years a high dependence on gadgets and may not reach his adult potential.

Access to Adult Predicaments

The information sites on the internet include many educational sites, but also the pornographic materials. As the teens are very curious and their sexuality is evolving, some of them use internet for locating exciting information and materials. Their premature exposure to pornographic materials on web sites may pose risks of various kinds. Adolescents unknowingly may come in contact with wrong people and enter pornographic chat rooms. Some of the available evidence suggested that (1) Peer to peer file-sharing networks is part of an all-pervasive sexualized media environment; (2) access to pornography and related sexual media can influence sexual violence, sexual attitudes, moral values and sexual activity of adolescents eroding morals. The more pornography the adolescents access, the higher the risk of their acting out what they see, including sexual assault.

A school counselor talked about the practice of using the internet for surfing pornographic materials to students of class VIII and IX in a government school. She found that a little over 40% had some knowledge about blue films and other materials on the internet. The percent of students in private schools exposed to these sites was much large.

For boys who are already at risk of anti-social behaviour, parents should carefully monitor and limit access to such sites. It has to be recognized that adolescents are not mere participants in this environment but they are actively shaping the nature of the environment itself. The excessive exposure to pornographic materials has been found to encourage a number of teens to transmit online sexually explicit pictures and videos of themselves/friends. Parents should supervise adolescents' media use and help teenagers to critique what they see in the media.

Many parents have lately heard about the new means of communication on the internet called cyber communities, such as, Orkut, Hi 5, Vital Reality, Facebook, MySpace, GTalk and Online Gambling. They recognize that these sites have a flip side, but only some block or monitor the use of these.

Orkut. Orkut is a social networking site that provides the facility of uploading 12 pictures in one's profile. Any person living anywhere can access these and make copies. This site is misused by some boys in reaching out to girls.

Nisha was a member of Orkut. She had put on it all her particulars her nature, interests, hobbies, phone no, e-mail and her photographs in various poses. One day a boy reached out to her through Orkut. He copied her photos and morphed them over nude bodies. He took her phone number from there and started blackmailing her. He wanted her to meet him lest he would show these photos to her parents and friends she had listed on the site. Nisha was quite upset. She could not talk to her parents about it. She confided ultimately in one of her teachers. The teacher listened to her narration about the obscene photos very patiently. She advised her to bring it to the notice of her parents and share her concerns with them. She also convinced her that the matter should be reported to police. Parents reported the case to cyber crime branch of police, who traced out the boy and took necessary action. Parents told Nisha in very definite terms to stay away from the site. Teacher spoke to the class and warned students of the dangers posed by such sites. Parents should caution their wards against putting their photographs, phone numbers and address. Now Orkut has a feature to lock the photographs.

MMS. This is another facility teenagers use on the cell phone to forward video clips and pictures and has been misused for sexual depiction.

Aadi, a student of class XI of a reputed public school was friendly with Ami, a girl in his class. They would spend lot of time together. He was able to persuade her to come to his house so that they could spend more time together. They would listen to music together and he would show her his e-creations with electronic gadgets. He had a lot of time and privacy with her at home as his parents were out at work for long hours. They started getting more intimate with each other and gradually started indulging in sexual activity. Aadi being a techno savvy boy, one day thought of recording their sexual relationship on his cell phone camera. He felt very thrilled about having these pictures on his cell phone. He forwarded the photographs to his friends to show his heroic deed.

This act became a big sensation for the class. Some students saw the photos and others wanted to see them too. Some felt that Aadi has cheated on Ami. When this came to the notice of Ami and her friends they felt very perturbed. The issue reached the class teacher. Seeing the magnitude of the problem the class teacher brought it to the notice of the principal. The Principal called the parents of both the kids. Ami's parents wanted the school to take a strong action against Aadi. Soon the news appeared in the media and became public. As the incident unfolded, it appeared that Aadi had not thought about the ugly consequences of it while planning the act. At that moment it was just the thrill of a smart use of technology. For many young teens, it became topic to gossip. School authorities had no choice as this act was awfully wrong. There was strong social and media pressure for punishing the boy. The school suspended the boy for two weeks who had to go through mandatory psychological examination, followed by professional counseling.

Some educationists and psychologists argued for a compassionate view, however. To them this act was done by a juvenile, who needed help. Aadi had not learnt to respect other people's privacy and dignity. He needed to learn that there are certain responsibilities that go with freedom. He came across as a lonely child who needed help in canalizing his knowledge of electronics into more creative and constructive uses. His parents provided him no support.

The case emphasized the need for all parents to discuss with their adolescents the danger of indulging into damaging activities with their techno skills and restraining their actions.

Chatting. Adolescents find chatting facility on internet quite an attractive element in social life. They chat with their friends and are able to reach out to new people sitting in another place (chat rooms). Adolescents can spend hours chatting with friends as this is an exciting experience for them and opens door to a new and larger world without any adult interference. They may learn many good things here and have a sense of enhanced self-confidence, but even the chatting facility has the possibility of being misused. Adolescents may come in contact with wrong people, like pedophiles and sexual predators, who use pornographic photos to pressurize their victims either to arouse a child or to lower a child's inhibitions and communicate that a particular sexual activity is okay: 'This person is enjoying it; so will you.' Adolescents often try to hide their identity as they are informed by their friends that they should not use their real name. They start using for themselves all sorts of names.

To attract boys to be friendly with her, 14 years old Malu named herself 'Glitter Girl' while another girl Soha kept her name as 'Pink Panty' without realizing what these names convey to others. Both girls were one day caught by their fathers while trying to keep a tab on their computer activities. Malu's father listened to her reasoning and shouted at her: Malu started crying and said that she had adopted this name seeing others keeping similar names. Soha on the other hand was a more stubborn girl. She reacted more strongly to her father's intruding on her privacy. She didn't want to talk about what she was talking and what name she adopted. Parents were concerned that she might get into some wrong trap, as already they heard her talking to boys at odd hours. The father just decided to block this facility on her computer. Soha was already having some behavioural problems and was visiting a counselor. Parents brought this behaviour also to the counselor's notice. The counselor discussed with Soha the different pros and cons of such indulgences related to sexuality, looks, physical and emotional changes.

There have been numerous instances of the misuse of chat portals. Many of the profiles are found fake and the intentions of people adolescents will be chatting with, are not known. Adolescents without knowing may come in contact with wrong people and enter pornographic chat rooms. The net savvy teenagers need to understand that pedophiles and sexual predators predominantly use internet to distribute child pornography materials and lure victims in chat rooms. In early and middle teens when sexuality is evolving girls often get lured into chatting with strangers. Parents have to talk to their adolescents cautioning them against using chat facility with strangers and getting into such traps.

Hacking/Plagiarism/Security Risks. There are some activities in cyberspace that may be undertaken by the skilled adolescents without being aware of the risky consequences. Some computer savvy and technically sophisticated adolescents may believe that they have an edge over others as they can use it for diverse purposes.

Amit, 16 years old is in class XI. He has been a good student so far, but not the topper kind. He loves playing with electronic gadgets. He can spend hours in taking them apart piece by piece and reassemble them. He started with small things like fixing irons, toasters and transistors and has graduated to fixing laptops and security systems. On his computer and cell phone, he is always busy getting into new sites, trying new games and programmes. One day he took his mother's customer ID and tried to log in her account without having her password. He wanted to make it work without asking his mother. He felt challenged and jumbled up several combinations of numbers based on the account number. He finally chose one number and was thrilled to find that it worked. Parents were surprised first but very upset later. They tried to make Amit understand its repercussions. They were very concerned about the bank security system, and have taken it up with the bank.

Teenagers like Amit however, need to know that hacking of sites is not risk free. It is considered now a computer crime.

The adolescents can use internet to disseminate their own creative work, which is an appropriate act, but some make its inappropriate use to disseminate copies of others' creative works and thereby infringe on copyrights, called plagiarism. Some online activities may look attractive but may make them vulnerable to security risks, like identity theft, spy ware and hacking. Online fraud and scams are seen now in many regions. Schools as well as parents need to teach the teenagers to use web and internet within the framework of cyber laws of the country, lest they may land in legal troubles and internet will lose its charm and utility for them.

Hate Campaign/Risky Groups. While communicating on the net adolescents are open to the risk of exposure to some online communities that support and advocate a variety of self-harm activities (suicide, anorexia, drug use) and try to self protect under the umbrella of group think phenomena. Such a group trap can be especially harmful for early and mid-adolescents. Adolescents, angry at their own conditions and failures may fall prey to either existing groups or form their own informal groups to vent anger and plan for disruptive activities. The hate groups can also use internet to post threats or distressing material as a 'joke' knowing fully its serious implications for the person.

After the Godhra riots in Gujarat, there were several hateful messages directed towards a particular community that appeared in the media and on a website. Aslam, a student of Class XI, came across this site and began to put messages on the web as rejoinders. Soon he began receiving between 5-10 rejoinders every day from students of other communities. It became a passion for him to send more and more hateful messages and also read equally abusive and hateful messages. After four months of doing this he was so depressed that he tried to burn a Hindu house in neighbourhood and commit suicide. Later, parents came to know what he has been going through. They took him for professional help.

Blog Writing. Blogs, often treated as the equivalence of online personal diaries, have become one of the fastest growing features of Web-based media. Persons write blogs on the web as blogging facilitates social networking and helps to conquer the distances to the known and the strangers. One can freely express opinions and emotions through blogs. In the blogosphere many communities have emerged, which include biased persons trying to express their views, or recruit new group members but also communities getting connected around issues of environment, social development and education etc. Adolescents write blogs and participate in regional and national affairs on subjects related to culture, language, fashions, and sports, and make their presence felt.

Manik, 15 years old said that 'I blog to share my views with others in different countries, and receive their views on my ideas and thoughts. This helps me in making new friends who have had similar experiences and opportunities. On blog now I can also post my pictures.' Kunal 18 years old has been writing blogs on marriages between higher caste and dalits on a debate carried out in a news magazine for a few months as it gives him a feeling of being a responsible human citizen. Sucheta 17 years old has been doing the same on position of women in the society. Hiren writes blogs on education to be made compulsory for all girls and boys in the country upto the age of 14 years. He enjoys the many rejoinders he receives as these are encouraging him to begin teaching school left-outs in his neighbourhood. If done in a good spirit, blogs can be effective means of sharing and helping people pursuing common interests.

Cell Phone Use

The number of cell phone users is exponentially rising in all age groups and most among the teens. One argument favouring its handing over to teens by parents has been of security. In case of both the parents working, it provides a means to remain connected to the child, or if a child is unwell or has to travel long distance, s/he can immediately call for help. However, the excessive use of it among children has come to pose discipline problems for the teachers and administrators in the school.

Cell has become a major source of distraction for the students as they use it mostly to network among friends more than anything else. They SMS their friends even during teaching hours. To deal with the issue schools have tried the practice of depositing the cell phones in the office on arriving in the school and collect it while going back home. It has added on to the responsibilities of the schools.

At home parents are getting worked up as the adolescents are using cell all the time, while studying, eating, resting and even at late hours in the night. There is no free time for the parents to talk to them.

Lovleen, 16 years old and a student of class XI has received a cell phone as a birthday gift from parents with clear instruction to use it to inform them once she has boarded the school bus from the bus stop, on reaching school, and on arriving back home. Additionally, she must call them if there is delay on the bus or she gets into difficulty somewhere. She kept her promise for a couple of weeks, and then she began using it for talking to friends and sending long text messages. Soon it was seen that she is communicating mostly with a boy friend Gautam, who does not have very good school records. One day while she was having lunch with the family her mother peeked into the message received. Lovleen tried to delete it but the language was so offensive that mother just snatched the cell from her hand and handed it to father. Lovleen got angry and threw her plate which invited the wrath of father. He got up from his chair, slapped her hard, took away the cell and called up Gautam's father. Gautam's father heard for a few seconds and then blamed Lovleen's father that if he is so concerned about his daughter, he should restrain her. She is the one spoiling his son. He also told him not to speak to him in future.

Lovleen's parents spoke to the class teacher and school counselor. The counselor told the parents about the need of monitoring the use of cell. They should not take away the facility but insist on its proper use and regulate it. They should also communicate with Lovleen and provide her psychological comfort to talk to them about her school friends and choice of entertainment etc. Once used to the facility, it will take some hard work for Lovleen and parents to get back to the habit of using it for necessary communication only and thus create the lost trust of each other. Both parties made efforts, and with periodical checks and intervention of the counselor the situation turned normal and healthy for Lovleen and parents.

Cell has become now a part of adolescents' lives. They are increasingly relying on it to define their identity and create social circles of their own. The trend will increase as cell phones morph into mini hand held computers and other sophisticated devices. More adolescents are going to ask for the cell and it is going to be difficult to deny them. What is required is to cultivate appropriate use habits. Parents should set the limit to the monthly cash card and the timing. While studying they should be encouraged to put it away. In the night a deadline may be mutually set. They should also be guided against the hazards and misuse.

Entertainment

Computers, Cell, TV, DVD, I-Pods and Video game devices use net technology for entertainment. Adolescents like to listen to music and find it very fulfilling because of their heightened emotionality. They like to have their own collection by downloading songs from the net, exchange it with friends or buy CDs. They listen to the music even when doing studies or other jobs. They love very loud music, which is irritating to most parents. Parents should give them adequate freedom but help them learn to respect others' privacy and responsible behaviour. Many teenagers, especially boys, use Console X box 30, Sony PS 3, mobile, online and video games and get carried away to continue playing for hours.

Vikky is 12 years old and is very fond of playing computer games. He has mastered the skill of playing these games and feels very thrilled on winning the game in a short time. He thinks this gives him an edge over his cousin who is not good at computer games. Soon Vikky began emulating the actions of the game in his daily life. Once he got angry on one of his classmates and boxed him hard. On coming home he told this to his mother and she was very upset. Many of these games glamourize violence impacting the impressionable minds of teens.

Every family uses TV/CD/DVD for entertainment within the comfort zone of their house. They watch movies, serials, live shows, sports, news etc. In some families TV is not turned off any time in the day and it distracts the children. The adolescents are the most vulnerable group. They get lured to its excessive use because of its audiovisual effects and easy accessibility. In schools teachers have reported TV as the major distraction to studies of students. The use of these devices can not be evaded but parents can take steps for promoting their use to the advantage of the adolescents. Parents can help them to develop healthy attitudes to use these with a balance in their daily schedules. Media also portrays stereotype roles and promotes certain products which indirectly influence the attitudes of teenagers. Parents and educators can help them develop healthy attitudes on issues such as gender roles and social responsibilities. Healthy discussions within the families can help children to shape their own perspectives. It may be good to make it a habit to watch with the children news at least once in a day.

Gadgets as Source of Family Discord

Many of the gadgets have become a source of conflict between parents and adolescents in many families. As the new models having more features appear in the markets, adolescents are tempted to get the latest model. They always want a model better than their friends so that they can show off. They constantly pressurize parents for it. Some get easily convinced that the cost does not warrant utility, whereas for others it may be an issue to brood.

Shobhit kept asking his parents for an I-Pod for two years saying that all others in his group have it. Finally parents decided to get him one after his class X exams. Parents gave the I-pod on the day of his results with lot of excitement, but the son showed a visible disappointment on his face. He would have liked a latest model since he was getting it after so long, for the parents though it was a huge sum to shell out. Similarly Ruchi a student of class XII told her parents 'I am not going to take this cell to the school after summer vacations. I think I need to change it. It really looks ancient.' Children not doing so well in other spheres seek recognition through expensive gadgets. A good parent child relationship can help adolescents to be more understanding.

Health Risks

There are many risks involved in the prolonged use of these gadgets as these emit radiations. Sitting for long in front of the computers can cause cervical and other postural problems. Children reading the computer screen continuously leads to dryness in eyes. This may affect the eyesight. Carpal tunnel a condition of the nerves of the wrist is known to occur with continuous keeping of the hand on the keyboard and mouse. Laptops kept on the lap emit radiation affecting reproductive organs. The adolescents' habit of continuously using mobile phones for long hours exposes them to radiation and can lead to cervical problems. It is not possible to deny the teens these gadgets, but parents can caution them against the health hazards. They should be encouraged to take breaks in between calls and avoid unnecessary use.

Conclusion. It seems obvious that net technology, internet and cell phones offer to the growing teens many opportunities, but these do not come free from dangers if used in an irresponsible fashion. The technology develops with promises and openings and does not focus on a specific age group. When adolescents use it they have to be guarded of the dangers ahead and use it with caution. Teachers have to set some guidelines, and parents have to carry the responsibility of monitoring the use, and of shaping their values around responsible citizenship. The use of Social Networking Sites like Web 2.0 is on the increase, but many times these sites are also misused. New security issues are thus surfacing. It is not possible to block all sites. It requires the development of values among adolescents to make proper use and effective parental monitoring.

TIPS FOR PARENTS AND TEACHERS

1. **Adult Involvement Desirable.** Adult involvement in the virtual world is very important. Share internet searching with adolescents. Teachers and parents should watch students' online activity and assign specific tasks using it. They should talk about the good and bad information that exists in the virtual environment. Encourage adolescents to talk about their experiences.

2. **Help Build Internal Resilience.** Teachers and parents may identify strategies that can help in building internal resilience in adolescents. They need to develop appropriate value oriented filtering and blocking mechanisms in the adolescent's behaviour.

3. **Develop Sense of Right and Wrong.** Adolescents need to develop a strong personal sense of right and wrong. It is better to empower the adolescents to build innate sense of right and wrong devoid of the threat of punishment or exposure.

4. **Teach Effective Search and Exit Strategies.** Adolescents need to be provided with instruction in effective search strategies and to learn how to quickly exit when they land in inappropriate sites.

5. **Understand the Harm Inherent to Actions.** Adolescents need to be encouraged to understand that their actions can cause harm. Parents and teachers should try to provide such an environment in which adolescents can freely share their feelings with them.

6. **Distribution as Harmful as Creating.** Adolescents need to be made aware that the distributing or forwarding of a harmful message is as inappropriate as composing it. They should think about the likely impact of their cyber communications on themselves, their friends and the virtual community.

7. **Place Computers in Shared Area.** Place computers in open and common areas that are easily visible to all.

8. Imbibe Safe and Ethical Practices of Use. Teachers, parents and administrators need to help adolescent users to imbibe such practices that would ensure cyber safety and ethical use. There is need of consciously talking about these to the young users.

9. Make Judicious Use of Time. Adolescents should learn time management along with opportunity to become techno-savvy. Other outdoor and creative activities apt for their age may also be pursued.

10. Teen Education Important. Teachers and parents have to educate the teens about thefts of e-mail addresses, data copying, removing of materials from the sites, and help them become responsible users of net technology. Inculcate the need and value of being cautious and safe.

8

Adolescent Communication

When people talk, listen completely. Most people never listen.

Ernest Hemingway

Communication Is a Need

Mahim (15 years), Mohan (16 years), Shreyas (18 years) love talking to their classmates and boys of their age in neighbourhood but not to parents and teachers. They all feel that parents are old to understand what, and why of their likes and dislikes and thus hardly a need to talk to them. Parents like to converse but often meet adolescents' reluctance. They all want to do away with the barriers in communication and yet find it difficult.

Communication is the essence of human life indeed. Persons in all age groups communicate with other person/s and the group/s for meeting their different needs, and experience a positive feeling. The transition from childhood to young adulthood changes for adolescents in many ways the contents and method of thinking, as their abstract and critical thinking have developed. They can process information faster and in qualitatively different ways. They communicate with peers much more closely than parents, teachers and others with whom they communicate only what is necessary. While they experience a feeling of joy in sharing their ideas with peers, often their manners and language alarm the adults. There is an increase in their ability to communicate, with simultaneous increase in the number of interpersonal conflicts at home and outside that block the available communication channels to them. The adolescents experience conflicts within themselves. They are expected to become independent but have the high pressure to communicate in socially acceptable ways. The conflicts with parents center around finances, appearance, family relations, school, curfew, friends, partying, smoking and drugs, and with teachers on academic work, regularity, punctuality and discipline. The conflicts with peers also emanate and remain centered on the tendency of trying to project oneself equal, and if possible a shade better than the other. The nature and type of communications adolescents have with their peers, teachers and parents affect their overall behaviour and well-being.

Communicating with Parents

The developmental period of adolescence is a temporary phase in life that comes to pass as they become mature, but challenging to families and to adolescents as well. As they grow, the sensitive issues of academic work, career, adventures, and the attention towards opposite sex come to surface. There is an increase in conflicts between parents and young adolescents. Families that have higher ability to change its power structure, role relationships and rules of relationship in response to the developmental demands, emotionally bond with each other well. This leads to positive developmental outcomes in adolescents, such as, school achievement, self-esteem, ability to resolve difficult life issues. Communication that is perceived as closed, conflict inducing, emotional, one-sided, or limited to certain topics convey to adolescents lack of trust, threat and rejection. It is believed that if adolescents can be helped to develop good communication skills, they can achieve positive self-image.

Although most adolescents are not happy when parents tell them what to do or not do, they understand and believe that parents care about them. They find that the expectations of appropriate grades, behaviour and adherence to rules parents set for them are positive but are neither realistic and nor clearly communicated to them. Parents need to be more consultative and extend their communications to cover diverse topics of interest to adolescents beyond academics and discipline. The discussions related to the forbidden subjects of sex, drug, alcohol and tobacco use, prior to exposure can increase the chances of adolescents' acting responsibly.

The exercise in communication starts from early childhood when parents play with the children, listen to their small talks, laugh and pat, and reinforce the appropriate behaviour. Children need to be given adequate opportunities to express themselves without inhibitions and to know basic information about their parents, like level of education, jobs and approximate incomes. There are many children who do not have knowledge of their parents' occupation and income. Some restructuring of parents' own timings may be necessary to be able to spend quality time with children. Some fathers seem to have minimal communication with children, especially the daughters.

The communication between adolescents and parents, and/or with other adults depends on their sense of mutual understanding and respect. Some parents have hard time in understanding the adolescent's need for privacy, and they want to know everything their teens think, plan and the details of persons they communicate with. Parents would do well indeed if they do not expect or pressurize their teens to share all thoughts or activities with them, although for safety reason they should always know where their wards are going, what they are doing and with whom, but they may abstain from muddling in details. Many of the TV shows, magazines and books, and the internet now provide access to tons of information, and parents need to stay aware of what the adolescent is watching and reading. Parents need to have faith in their teen as much as they desire teens to have faith in them, and occasionally reward him/her for being trustworthy. It is important for parents to remember that adolescents are living in a highly complex and technology oriented world. They face pressures of a different hue than encountered by the earlier generations, and have to learn the needed skills to live effectively now and be prepared to cope future challenges.

Communicating with Teachers

Adolescents communicate with teachers in the formal and highly structured school setting. It makes the communications by nature systemic and limited to issues of curriculum, performance, participation in extra-curricular activities and discipline. Good communication between student and teacher would facilitate learning and prevent students from having many behavioural problems. Such a relationship may act as a buffer against the ups and downs of growing up in their teen years. A strict disciplinarian teacher conveys knowledge but there is no guarantee that students will receive it. Teachers allowing students to have space for questioning and discussion usher for them new freedom of self-expression. Such teachers are easily approachable, and encourage students to open up their diverse concerns.

The communications between the teachers and students may vary because of personal like and dislikes, differences in backgrounds, the way teacher responds to male or female students or any other personal biases. Teachers' own communication skills, acceptance of diverse behaviours and personal interest in students may promote better interactions in the classroom. The communications also depend on the personal factors of the student, the structure of the classroom e.g. number of students in the class, variables implicit in the teaching-learning roles and the structure of lessons. Teachers need to set high but realistic standards as too high expectations tend to frustrate students leading to the avoidance of academic work. This becomes over time a source of conflict between the students and teachers, and may extend to parents. A teacher having good communication skills can reach out to students having diverse needs and stimulate them.

Adolescents who remain deficit in communication skills may have some negative factors either related to their personal predispositions or context, and/or both.

Personal Predispositions

The personal predispositions may be of shyness, emotionality and lack of self-confidence.

Shyness. Shivam, a student of class XI showed severe problems related to his communication skills. Despite the fact of being a good student he had difficulty in asking his teachers for help in studies and school programme. He felt very shy and could not dare to stand up in the class to ask any question. Whenever teachers asked him a question, he would answer in monosyllabic words. He had good academic background and comprehension ability, but was not able to communicate clearly even about the things he knew very well.

When Shivam was in junior classes he was reasonably comfortable, but as he proceeded to higher classes he started having class adjustment problems. In the middle school, it was seen as a matter of routine that other boys will take away his things or borrowed his notebooks etc. and he would readily give them. But when he needed reciprocal help from them, they would somehow manage to escape and not do things for him. At times, boys would even tease him and make fun of him. He did not report it to the teacher and did not know how to cope with this behaviour of other boys. He started feeling unhappy in the class and school as well. He often complained about it to his parents and wanted them to sort this out for him. He felt awkward about it, when parents came to the school, as no other child asked parents to intervene. He graduated from class X with average results.

In class XI onwards his studies deteriorated further. Parents were very concerned about it. They sent him for science and maths group coaching, but he could not adjust in the coaching class. He would not ask for needed help and clarifications in front of others, as he had difficulty in speaking in the group situation. He started missing the classes. He felt he was not benefiting and decided to leave the coaching class. Shivam came from a well to do family and was the only child. Parents over protected him, but in a bid to help him achieve perfection, they checked him for everything as a routine. With passing years they became over critical of him—'this is not the way to eat, this is not the way to meet people', became an all time routine. Soon he started feeling that he cannot manage anything on his own. He lost self-confidence and detested meeting people. Shivam developed lot of negative feelings about himself, which affected his communication skills and thereby his social and academic skills.

The case shows that Shivam was shy, self-conscious and not used to dealing with more people at home. Being the only child he was over protected, his needs were well met and he was the focus of attention. Perhaps getting things without asking, he never learnt the skill and confidence to talk and request others for help. A very high degree of control of parents on his activities made him lose self-confidence and set in negative feelings towards self. He struggled to find his place in the group and at home, in a way his personal identity. Thus shyness, lack of confidence, and negative self-image may become a barrier in communication of adolescents with others, affecting other areas of development and adjustment beyond studies in social and extra-curricular activities.

Assertiveness-A Growing Up Need. Rajeev was a 16 years old middle class family boy. As he grew into middle adolescence, his parents felt that he was becoming increasingly rude to family members. He snapped back on little things and wanted no checks on his activities. The parents did not understand how to deal with him. Till a few years back he used to be a very obedient and well behaved child. They were worried if he was on the wrong track or would develop into an ill mannered person. They talked, about this newly developed behaviour of Rajeev, to some close friends who suggested that they better consult his school counselor.

As parents were really worried they met the school counselor. They reported—'these days Rajeev remains confined to self. He has totally withdrawn from others. Whatever we say he gets irritated. All the time he wants to be with his friends. He is O.K. with them, laughing, joking, and giggling. He either goes out with his friends or remains in his room. But with us he is very rude, snappy, and impatient.' They narrated a sample of conversation between them and Rajeev, which is reproduced below:

> He says 'I can't sit with you.' When we go to his room he says—'Please don't come in my room all the time.

Can't you leave me alone for some time?' The moment we try to talk to him about anything, he says 'What do you want. I have had enough of lecture.' While going out he does not tell where he is going. When we ask him, his reply is 'I don't know when I will come back.' Or 'Don't ask me. Why do I have to tell you everything like a small child?' All the time it is 'My friends, my friends....' If we say anything about eating, or meeting relatives or going out, his reply is 'You do not know anything about present times. You are so backward.' 'Other children's parents do not keep as much check as you people. I feel so suffocated in this house.'

Mother said—I have tried to explain to him so many times 'you are not so grown up that you can decide everything on your own. We are concerned about you.' The answer comes 'Ma, leave that crap.' Mother said I often insist that 'you need to think about your future career. Your father thinks you should start preparing for engineering entrance. You are not taking it seriously.' Instead of listening the reply comes, 'Why should he think and decide for me. I will see what I want to do. May be I will do Eco. Honours. I will see after finishing class XII what to do.' After a few days when his father again reminded him of engineering coaching, Rajeev slammed the door and said—'You have only one thing to talk.'

The counselor made the parents understand and appreciate that Rajeev is a sensible boy. He wants his space and wants to make his own decisions. The teenager is searching for his own identity and desires independence. They would do well by discussing things in a mature manner and respect his decisions rather than imposing their ideas on him. There needs to be more discussion, consultation, recognition of strengths and weaknesses of Rajeev as a teen. They were reassured that giving the child more privacy and independence will not spoil him. It would rather help him in developing self-confidence and self-identity.

Often parents regard the need for assertion as being rude and indisciplined. This may result in sharp exchanges between them and threaten their relationships. Parents should try to understand the needs of adolescent in their exercise of control, lest it may lead to aggression.

Context Factors

Differences in Perspectives. Some of the factors underlying inadequate communication between adolescent and parents or/and other adults are seen related to differences in their levels of education, intellectual functioning and aspirations. Adolescents were indeed quite conscious of it and found it apt to talk during a group session between a school counselor and class XI students on the topic of relationships and communication in the family. A large number of students had the feeling that their parents did not understand them because of differences in their education etc. A good number confessed that they hardly converse with fathers.

One such case is of a girl, named Sushila. She came from a lower middle class household. Her father worked at a store, and was educated only up to middle school. She said—'I do not talk to my father. There is no time to talk to him. He comes home very late and then he says he is very tired. At that time I am generally helping my mother to make the food or doing my studies. If my younger siblings talk to him he gets very angry. My mother tells them not to disturb him as he comes back home after full day of work'. Sushila further told, 'Ma'am my father is very hot tempered. I feel scared to talk to him. Early in the morning we come to the school having no time to say anything to him.' She did not know anything about his work.

She also had limited interaction with mother. 'I talk to her, but only about the routine things. She does not understand most things. She is very old fashioned. She wants me to sit at home, do household work and wear old fashioned clothes only. She does not want me to go out or meet friends. In fact, my level of thinking is completely at variance with that of my parents. Whenever I have to share my feelings, I talk to my friend Saloni in the school. Many times I have to tell lies to my mother about what I want. At times I shout at her when she does not understand. Then she gets angry and tells me that I am becoming very rude and obstinate these days.' There was no going out as a family. Parents were completely unaware of the needs of their growing up children.

Like Sushila, many other students at school got better exposure and their thinking developed. This further widened the gap between them and the parents especially in case of socially deprived families with parents being less educated, conservative, not giving time and deliberately trying to impose their wishes undermining adolescent needs. They need to consciously set certain time in a day to talk to them to know about their friends, studies, various activities and experiences in the school and/or do some activities together at home. This would give all of them opportunity for better communication and thus better understanding. Teachers working with underprivileged children may guide parents in this direction.

Parental Attitudes. Deepa was a class XII commerce student. She had been so far an all round good student in the school. Everybody in the school had placed her quite high in their expectations and assessment. One day two of her friends brought her to the school counselor saying that she has some serious problem. The counselor looked towards her and she started crying. She said 'Ma'am I can not continue with my studies. I think I should drop this school year.' Deepa continued, 'Ma'am, my mother is not keeping well. She is on bed most of the time. Being a girl I have to look after her and have to do all the household work. There is also pressure of studies. The Board exams are coming. I have to go for Accountancy and Maths tuitions in the evening. There are class tests every second day in the school. I do not know how to cope. Please advise me what should I do? Should I drop a year?'

The counselor explored for information about her family and support system available at home. She said she has at home her father and an elder brother. The brother is learning computer programming and doing graduation privately. The counselor further asked 'have you discussed all this with your father and brother? Yes Ma'am, I have tried several times. But they repeatedly tell me that you are a girl. You are supposed to do all household work. My father scolds me if household work is not done by the time he comes back from work.' When I said more forcefully, he even raised his hand on me a couple of times saying 'you have even started arguing with me. You have become very rude these days'. While talking about this, she started crying and got very upset. She said, 'Ma'am, my life is worse than an animal. Nobody understands me at home and/or is concerned about my feelings, my career and my life.' The counselor asked her, 'Have you shared your feelings with your friends or teachers?' 'Yes Ma'am, with my very close friends. I haven't told the teachers as I don't like bringing family problems to the teachers. It will spoil my image in their eyes.'

The counselor further explored—'What about your brother? Have you asked him to share work with you?' 'Yes. He says like father that it is your work.' The counselor asked, 'Doesn't your father say anything to him.' 'No Ma'am. The brother has lot of time at his disposal. When he comes home, father asks him about his studies and the progress in the computer class?' To me it is always—'you can do it later on. First look after the household chores. In his free time, brother is allowed to go out to meet his friends. Other day when I was coming back from the Accountancy Tuition, I was with my classmates. There were some boys and girls with me. My brother passed by. On coming home he reported this to father. Again I got the scolding from father that I was having nice time and why was I with boys all the time. Then even I got angry.' The counselor consulted her subject teachers. They had observed a drop in her class performance. They had also tried to ask her the reason but she avoided talking about it.

To help Deepa, the counselor asked her to write down her feelings. This gave vent to her pent up feelings which she was not able to express to others. She was given assurance about her capabilities and strengths, and encouraged to cope with the circumstances. She was given tips on time management. She was also helped to express her own feelings to others at home in a more acceptable manner. Some of the ways to seek help from others were discussed with her.

With her consent, her brother and father were called to the school separately. The counselor told the brother, how Deepa has been feeling about her studies and home pressures. He was told that Deepa had always been a very good student, but now because of work overload at home she was thinking of dropping the year. With his cooperation and support, her year can be saved. Initially, he also expressed his reactions and irritations against her, but later on he agreed to give her a helping hand. In subsequent sessions, Deepa reported that her brother has become more considerate and was sharing some work with her.

The father was called to the school on another pretext and suggested that Deepa needed more time for studies at home as the Board exams were approaching. This made him think to arrange a helping hand at home and call some female relative to stay with them for some time. Deepa started looking more relaxed. She had a big smile on her face when a few days later she met the counselor. Her aunt has come to stay with them for some time. She got more support and understanding from the father now. Deepa gave her class XII exams and passed with good marks.

Apparently, Deepa was not able to communicate her needs and feelings to her family members. In the family, the female was placed on a lower pedestal and her education had lower priority. There were stereotypical roles identified and valued for females, like household work, care of sick mother etc. Males were not to share the work, which was a big pressure on Deepa in finding time to study. There was lack of effective communication alongwith lack of understanding between family members. She did not share her problems with any of the teachers in school as she was trying to hold to the image of a brave girl and also thought that family concerns are not to be shared with anybody though she had excellent rapport with the teachers. Being a diligent girl she was trying to do everything on her own beyond her capacities. She shared her feelings only with friends who have been very supportive of her. The counselor was able to help her by talking to the brother and father.

The parental attitudes towards adolescents affect the type of communication in the family. Teachers can play a positive role here by identifying the students having problems and encouraging them to share their problems. Teachers can also influence parents to change their rigid attitudes and develop better communication and understanding with family members.

Parents Short of Time and Comparing with Others. Some adolescents have well-off parents but they do not have time for children.

Suchita is 16 years old and a student of class X in a private school. She is intelligent and scores above 70% in most subjects. Her family is quite affluent. Father is a business executive and mother teaches in a college. She has her grandmother and maid staying at home. Once she comes from school, she is in her room listening to music or is busy on phone. She does not talk much to her grandmother. Parents come home in the evening and hardly talk to anyone. When they try to find out something, she refuses to talk about school work or friends. A few sample conversations are reproduced below:

> On one Sunday Suchita was asked by her mother what she planned to do during the day. Suchita said she wants to visit a friend. This angered mother and she said—'You do not have time for us. All the time you are with your friends. Once in a while, you should also sit at home.' The father told her in a sharp tone—'You have to be home today.' She slammed the door and went to her room.' The mother went to her room wanting to talk to her daughter and said—'What Anjali tells you is O.K. with you but what I tell you is always wrong. What Anjali wears you want to wear the same. Wherever she goes, you want to go. When will you develop your own thinking? You should listen to me. I am fed up with you.' This evoked negative responses in Suchita rather than listening to what the mother was trying to tell her.

The mother was often impatient in dealing with her daughter and compared her with her close friends 'you are copying Ridhi all the time. You should even study like her. See, she scored so well. She even got prizes in elocution and games.' The mother commented without realizing the strengths and weaknesses of her daughter. The obvious reply of the daughter was—'You always like other children. I am always bad for you.' The mother at another time said, 'I do not like your friend Madhu. I don't like the way she talks. You should remain with Ambika. She is a nice girl and comes from a good family.' But Suchita was friendly with Madhu as to her Ambika was more arrogant and she would not value Ambika's opinion, whereas with Madhu, she had more in common and liked her company. Now Suchita stopped talking about her friends to the mother.

Long phone calls to friends made her parents upset. Parents often commented—'You have been on the phone for last one hour. You were with your friends in the school for more than six hours. What is there to talk to them for so long again in the evenings.' Such remarks made Suchita angry and had no effect on her, resulting in repeating the same act next day.

The case of Suchita demonstrated how the communication between the teenager and parents operated at tangents with each other. Parents telling her made no difference or evoked angry reactions. The teenagers detest being told what to do and not to do. They hate sharp criticism of themselves, their friends, clothes, mannerism and behaviour. When parents become insensitive to feelings of growing children, it provokes them to react. Either they withdraw from parents completely or become aggressive in their assertions with them. They start hiding things and talking back in high tone. The peer group is very important to teens. The tilt towards the peer group makes the parents feel that the teen is drifting away from them. This evokes variety of reactions in parents. Parents need to be more understanding and encouraging to their teens. They should be receptive and may try to facilitate two way communications.

More freedom for trivial things and better listening to what the teenager wants to say is needed.

The case showed that parents communicate with their wards in a way that there is no meaningful sharing. There is emphasis on school and studies, but no supportive attitude or desire to engage in details. The absence of healthy communication between parents and teens has not allowed the development of mutual understanding and trust.

Nowadays many more women work in demanding jobs and have little time for their adolescents. On returning home they feel stressed out and impatient. The adolescents are at a very crucial juncture of life and need their parents most for sharing their experiences, have support and reassurance for their behaviour. Parents need to make a conscious effort to take time out for their wards. They may reschedule their activities and keep some time for common programmes with their wards.

Severe Communication Problems

Some adolescents have difficulty in making friends and thus have limited communication.

Radhika was a student of class IX in a private school. She did not have friends in neighbourhood, nor was she liked by other students in the school. She was labeled a fighter and most students avoided her. She was jealous of other girls who were friendly with each other. Other students called her names like 'Poison' 'cobra' etc. She would always complain to teachers about others, but she was not taken seriously. Radhika told her parents about it. She wished she too was like other girls who had many friends and were popular. She also brought this to the notice of the counselor.

Mother also had problems with her. One day she complained to the counsellor, 'All the time Radhika does what she wants to do and does not listen to anybody. She does not like being told about doing her studies. The type of food she wants to eat, the clothes and the beauty aids she wants to use, the amount of money she wants to spend, the long phone calls, the electronics she wants to possess are constant source of conflict with us. We are very concerned that she is not doing her studies. She was either failing or just getting through in all the subjects. Whenever we tell her anything she replies back in harsh tone. She has stopped talking to me (mother). Very often she tries to create misunderstandings between me and her father. Both of us are scared of her. We do not check her for anything now, as she has started threatening us that she will run away from home if not allowed to do things her way. She is also friendly with some boys to whom she makes long phone calls or communicates through internet. She even chats with unknown people.'

This case shows that Radhika had severe problems in relating with others. She has not learnt to get along with people. In fact, she stayed away from her parents in her formative years and came to live with them when she was nearly 11 years old. Thus she did not develop understanding with her parents and the gap increased gradually. She has not learnt to interact with known people and strangers in a healthy manner. She thinks that she can get the attention of others by creating fights between them. All her irritation and anger arises from the need for recognition. She was feeling left out everywhere. Her academic records were not good either. Neither she had excelled in any co-curricular activity or chose any hobby. Unfortunately teachers and parents did nothing to help in developing her communication skills. Teachers took more or less a prejudiced view based on what others said about her and parents did little. She was getting negative reinforcement from people around her and had low self-esteem.

Radhika required professional help. Her underlying need of recognition and overall adjustment may be addressed. Reinforcement may be given for the correct use of language and behaviour. She needs reassurance and acceptance from the people around to develop her self-esteem and confidence. She may require long term training in building communication skills and relationships, like listening, sensitivity to others, helpfulness and trust building.

Healthy Communication

Some adolescents are lucky to have very good interactions in the home and outside. Bela and Beeru are the two siblings in a progressive public school. For the school PTA meeting each student was asked to write a message for their parents. Bela, 13 years old, wrote 'My parents are very supportive. I can confide in them for anything and everything.' Beeru 9 years, wrote 'You are so good. I love you s-o-o-o-much.' Their message was highlighted by their class teachers as an indicator of the good relationship between children and parents.

The mother Mrs. Soni worked in R&D department of a multinational company. When her children were young, she arranged with her husband that she would go to office ahead of him and would be back by 4.00 o'clock. Her husband went late to the office and stayed late in the evening. Mr. Soni took care of children's bath, breakfast and school going. After coming home Mrs. Soni escorted the children to the park and played with them. She would read out stories to them while serving dinner. The father would put them to sleep after coming back from office. After children went to sleep by 8.00 o'clock, they had ample time even for themselves.

As the children grew up and started going to school, their mother's coming home from office at 4.00 o'clock was a happy time for children. They had finished their homework by then. While she relaxed and had her cup of tea, children would tell her their full day's stories, experiences and excitements and did extra studies. In the evening children were left to play with their friends. Thrice a week, children went for hobby classes, and mother took time to meet her friends, to read or go for household purchases. The father liked playing cricket or board games with children. The weekends were used for going out together to parks, educational places, museums or meeting family friends. Parents watched and discussed the TV programmes with children. There was plenty of laughing and joking in the house. Parents had lot of interaction with children while stimulating their mind for learning and developing opinions on various issues.

As Bela was in her teens, Mrs. Soni made it a point to give her some personal time to satisfy her queries about her friends and newly formed relationships particularly with boys. She would listen to Bela with understanding but without being judgmental. During these conversations the mother got the opportunity to guide her without sounding like lecturing the daughter. Bela found her mother more of a friend and confidant. With the mother, Bela would talk about clothes, what suited her best and what was in vogue. Girls of her age normally look for reassurance which she got from her mother. Bela would listen to her suggestions. The mother would say things in a suggestive manner and not in an authoritarian way. She would give her choices—'this will be better for you' or 'you decide out of these two.' Plenty of freedom was given to children but limits were set. For disciplining them pros and cons of actions were told rather than straight 'no'.

Bela was very good in studies, but Beeru was not so good. No comparisons were made between the two children. Rather, each one's strengths were recognized and encouraged. Parents did not have undue expectations from them, nor set very high targets for them. In the type of family environment Bela had, all adolescents would perhaps feel free to come to their parent for any problem.

In another case, Vaibhavi a 17 years old from a middle class family, came home from school feeling very excited. As she entered the house, she called 'Ma, Ma, where are you? I have to tell you something. Today, after exam we went to Khan market. Though we are not allowed to miss our school bus we did it today. We wanted to have fun. 6-7 of us roamed around in the market and had burgers at McDonald. It's so cool. Reema and I have come back with Keshav in his car.'

Her mother did not react to the situation. She said 'It's O.K. for once. Good you told me, but it is always good to adhere to school norms. You may get into trouble sometime. I do not want any unpleasant situation for you.' Vaibhavi threw the school bag on her bed, while still talking to mother. She sat on the bed and said 'Ma, I have to talk to my friend about some school gossip about Reema.' Mother asked 'what's it about?' Vaibhavi said—'No Ma, I can not tell you. It's about Shouvik and Reema. I want to ring up my friend. I have to tell her everything. Please can you leave me alone. I will tell you later on.' The mother left the room giving the daughter her privacy. She realized that at this age adolescents like to share the crushes, attractions or relationships in their own age group.

After half an hour or so Vaibhavi came out of her room calling for mother again. 'Ma, I have to miss my dance class today. My friends are coming over in the evening. We want to have a party and chill. You better be at home. You know that they love talking to you and Dad. Tanuj loves discussing things with Dad.' The mother told Vaibhavi—'But there is very little time for preparation. You have got to help me. Yes, Ma, after I have rested.' The mother prepared food and snacks for them. Vaibhavi helped her in preparing snacks and setting the room. In the evening, after 7.00 o'clock her friends started coming in batches. They met Vaibhavi's parents and chatted with them off and on. After some time, the parents went out to call on some friends giving the teens their freedom. Later on they joined them for dinner for a while.

Vaibhavi's case showed perfect rapport between her and her parents. They were conscious that Vaibhavi was an average student but showed no over concern in their interactions. They wanted her to develop other personality traits that will help her in the long run. They recognized that teens like having fun and adventures, but they also encouraged her cooperation in the house. Understanding of teenage needs is important. Parents have to maintain balance between freedom and control. Good communication is required between them to be able to understand and guide them. They need trust and confidence in each other.

Do's for Parents

1. Be Patient. Recognize that all behaviour is communication. 'When Rita told to her parents I don't want to talk, slammed the door and walked away shrugging her shoulders, she communicated a lot.' You need to be patient to respond and not show your helplessness by over reacting. You may also look at her non-verbal communication.

2. Be a Good Listener. Ask yourself 'Do I listen to my teen?' and 'Do I accept her/his different tastes and opinions.' Listen to them in a non-judgmental manner and show more understanding. Remember that imposing of adult views on adolescents distances them.

3. Spend Time. Spend some quality time with your teens and listen to their stories, experiences of school and friends, how they spend time etc. This conveys the feeling that we care.

4. Show Openness. Be more open and share some memories of your adolescence with your teens. Encourage them to share their concerns without hesitation. Over nagging and/or being over protective both are detrimental to good relationships. Keep your communication a two-way process. Have good equation with your adolescent, even if it is not in line with your value system. Set limits, but remember too strict a rule, and executing control become barriers in communication.

5. Be Creative. Think what will work and do to get moving on. One can be casual and not take things personally. Add a sense of humour, mirror the adolescent, try self-disclosure or give an example out of your experience to break the ice and laugh together.

6. Empathy. Be empathetic to make them accept that it's normal to be self-conscious, but do not be self-centered.

7. Encourage Friends. Encourage adolescents to make friends right from childhood. One feels lonely without friends. Allow them to spend time and share feelings with friends. The development of good relationships is an evolving process. Having faith, trust, giving support, maintaining confidentiality, and giving compliments nurture friendship.

8. Accept Others. Help them to develop positive attitudes towards others. The negativity and criticism of others promote withdrawal from people.

9. Freedom of Choice. Right from childhood give your teen freedom to make own decisions. Respect their likes/dislikes and opinions to enhance their self-confidence and self-esteem.

Enable them to stand and speak for their own rights in a polite manner without evoking reactions in others.

10. Good Language. Use appropriate language and expression in your communication with adolescents. An adolescent who sees his parent shouting and screaming or using foul language may use same behaviour in a similar situation.

11. Give Responsibility. Teach teens dignity of labour irrespective of own socio-economic status. Give them specific responsibilities, like cleaning and decorating their room. Involve them in making preparations for special occasions or festivals etc.

Suggestions for Teachers

1. Be Open and Accepting. Be open and make students feel comfortable. Make them feel accepted and appreciate whatever good they do. Evolve a relationship of respect, understanding and be there whenever needed.

2. Get Rid of Biases. Shed your personal biases, inhibitions and prejudices. Make all students feel equal, enjoying fairly compatible opportunities of learning and growth, irrespective of gender, caste, socio-economic status etc. Do not avoid talking directly to a troubled or trouble making student.

3. Be Helpful. Be proactive and always ready to help students in resolving emotional, financial and social issues.

4. Know Families. Maintain contact with families of students.

5. Show Concern. Make teens understand that teachers like parents are concerned about them. They care and feel hurt. They too have their happy and sad moments. Do with them role reversal exercises to make them understand how distorted interactions can occur between people and how important it is to keep in view the others' perspectives to interactions.

9

Behavioural Issues

How much more grievous are the consequences of anger than the causes of it.

Marcus Aurellus

Hardly two days in a row pass and one comes across one behavioural incident or the other involving school adolescents making news in the media. Some of these are of extreme type involving grievous injury or killing, such as shooting, suicide, and road rage. Some others are less dangerous and amenable to positive change, like indulgence in goofing up, defying rules and lying. These affect every day life of many adolescents and adults around. An increase in the incidence of such events has heightened the concerns of parents, school administrators, educators and professionals working with adolescents.

Exercising Independence

Many of the behavioural issues arise from the gap between the heightened adolescent needs of gaining autonomy and social recognition, and the available opportunities for the expression of these in their social context. One's stepping into adolescence sets in her/him an intense desire to exercise independence and push most bars to social and family norms. Conflicts and confrontations are inbuilt in the process. Some parents and adolescents come to hold perspectives wide apart from each other and remain at logger heads. Same is true of the relationship with teachers. Adolescents want to take control of their lives and activities. They want to exercise their independence by questioning the rules set by parents and others in authority like teachers, which may lead to rule breaking. Parents and teachers may not consider each rule breaking incident worthy of punishment. They need to differentiate between occasional errors of judgment they may make and a misbehaviour that may require punitive measures or professional intervention. For example, frequent eve-teasing, bullying, fighting, truancy and theft may be considered much more significant than isolated episodes of the same activities.

It is a normal behaviour for all adolescents to get involved in occasional physical fight with their siblings/peers, but when the frequency and intensity increases to the extent of hurting the sensibilities of another person, it may have to be considered a problem. Although incidents of severe physical fights at school nowadays make news in media, adolescents may be involved in close to similar fights in the neighbourhood and outside school. Many factors, including developmental issues, group membership, substance use, poverty, living in proximity of anti-social elements and access to weapons, can contribute to an increased risk of violence. Those subjected to harsh punishment and cruelty are more likely to indulge in crimes. Of particular concern are adolescents who in an altercation tend to lose self-control and cause serious injury with or without a weapon.

As adolescents are more independent and mobile than children, they are out of the direct physical control of adults. Their behaviour is determined by their own moral and behavioural codes. The parents may guide rather than try to directly control the adolescents' actions. Adolescents enjoying the warmth and support, care and supervision of parents are less likely to engage in risky behaviours. Same is true of those who are clearly told what is expected of their behaviour, have consistent limits set and monitoring is done of their activities. Parents who believe in consulting their wards for setting the rules and practices are most likely to display positive behaviours. Such parents tend to use a system of reinforcement in which they give to their ward at one time small bits of responsibility and freedom. When they find that the adolescent has acted in a responsible manner for quite some time they give more freedom. They also deal with the abuse of freedom by reducing the incentives/privileges. Parents do so to remind their ward that they set rules. The adolescents are expected to take advantage of parents through their positive actions (by attending school, complying with houschold responsibilities), than showing off (dress, hair style, preferred entertainment). Adolescents who continue to show despite their parents' best efforts, incompliance or otherwise unacceptable behaviour may need help.

Signals for Behavioural Issues

Some warning signs for the behavioural issues that parents may need to watch are— extreme weight gain or loss, sleep problems, rapid and drastic changes in personality, sudden change in friendships, skipping school on a regular basis, falling grades, talk or even jokes about suicide, signs of tobacco or drug use and run-ins with the law agencies. The behavioural issues may range from mild to serious as discussed here:

Defying Rules

Teenagers may resort to it as a fun activity to begin with.

Sheeba and Mira the two class IX girls, on last Monday after the school did not board the school bus. They called their parents and informed that they have an extra class in the school. Instead they went to see a movie with two boys. On coming home they did not tell parents anything. They ate and went to their rooms. Again this week they repeated the same excuse and went to a restaurant with the same boys. They again got away. They kept going out like this till one day one of the neighbours saw them coming out of a restaurant and mentioned it to the mother of one of the girls. The parents felt very angry at this behaviour and they were both grounded at home and not sent to the school for few days. This led to some behavioural problems even at home. They would be on the phone most of the time, sleep for long hours, pick up fights with family members and do no studies. Parents laid down certain rules about how they should spend their time and made schedule for the day, but of no avail. Invariably, they would snap back on the parents or end up in long arguments. They started locking their rooms from inside so that others do not get a wind of their activities. Then one day their class teacher rang up the parents to know why the girls were not coming to the school. The parents told the reason. The class teacher asked the parents to come with the girls to the school to meet her at the earliest.

The parents brought the girls to the school the following day and met the class teacher. The class teacher explained to the parents that at this age the adolescents have other needs too. It is natural for girls and boys to enjoy the company of opposite sex. Also this age is characterized by the desire for freedom and having adventures. Thus certain amount of freedom should be granted to them but limits should be set. In a week, some mutually agreed time should be allotted to them to meet their friends, to go out, have other activities and to enjoy. The parents were suggested that they allow other adolescents, inclusive of boys, to come to their house in the evenings so that they develop healthy interactions. The girls were also told that defying the rules and telling lies can lead to serious problems in life. Schools and parents set certain rules which are for their welfare.

This is a typical example of very strict parents, who set very high goals for their ward without realizing their evolving needs and not involving them in setting these. In such cases adolescents try to cope by defying rules at home and school, and telling lies. Parents need to be more sensitive and understanding of the teenager's needs in setting expectations and limits.

Truancy. It is more common among boys, although girls may indulge too.

Suresh and Mohan, two students of class XII in a private school in South Delhi hatched a plan to escape their term exam in science. Suresh called up Mohan's parents in the afternoon of the exam day that Mohan came to his house and as they were walking outside the home, two unknown persons encountered them and took away Mohan in a gypsy. While going they asked him to inform Mohan's parents about it if he wants his safety. Parents called up the police. The police got into action and found Mohan sitting in a fast food joint enjoying his snack. The police questioned him and came to know that this boy planned his own kidnapping as he would not be able to pass his exam and meet his parents' expectations.

The principal referred Mohan to the school counselor and asked parents to meet her. The counselor found that parents had very high expectations of Mohan which he could not achieve. They were advised to set their expectations realistically and also to keep an eye on his peers and their movements. She explained that many adolescents are not able to cope with the school teaching when they have to satisfy very high expectations of self/parents/teachers, have fear of punishment or find the school teaching uninteresting. They develop feelings of shame/guilt that cause anxiety. In a bid to get rid of anxiety they go away and avoid studies. Many miss school by going to a movie, sitting in the parks or roaming around for days. Some resist getting up in the morning on some pretext and avoid going to school. This annoys most adults, but they need to understand the situation in order to deal better with it.

Similar are the cases of adolescents who find the home or the social environment non-conducive due to parental abuse, alcoholism etc. and run away (found on railway stations and markets etc.).

Lying

A lie is a deliberate falsehood communicated with the intention to mislead or deceive. The conflicts between parental control and personal autonomy may lead to adolescent lying. They do so to get power from parents and other authority figures. It hurts parents' feelings when they find the adolescent is lying to them. To the adolescent this feeling of hurt or anger proves that they are no more controlled by parents. Adolescents may also lie to cover up other problems like, illicit drug or alcohol abuse. Early parental intervention in such situations is needed to prevent the formation of the habit of lying.

Harinder is just 14 and is finishing class VIII exams in a private school. His family is forward looking in some ways and very conventional in others. His parents go to clubs, and often return late at night leaving him to the care of a servant. Harinder remains home and often gets bored. Now he has begun to go out with friends and lies to parents that he studied while they were away. Or he uses the servant to get food, cigarettes etc. from outside, and bribes him to not to report to the parents. He keeps on taking money out of mother's purse and never accounts. When parents ask him he lies that he was busy in studies. One day he invited his two friends and asked the servant to get in addition to food and cigarettes some beer. He again bribed the servant to not tell it to parents. When parents came back he again lied that he had been studying only. This practice continued till one day father discovered that Harinder has drank so much that next morning he missed the school.

A couple of weeks later the parents received a note from the principal that Harinder was not coming to school regularly and they must meet her. They went to the school and talked to the principal and counselor. The counselor explained that they should not ignore Harinder. When Harinder is lonely, he indulges in activities that they do in clubs etc. They have to be sensitive to his needs. By doing so he is trying to say 'I feel lonely', 'Even I want to have fun', 'I want to experience new things,' 'I am no more a baby' and so on. They must spend time with him and eat dinner together as much as possible. Some better alternatives need to be provided to him like reading an exciting book while they are away from home, or inviting his friend over to spend the night. It may also require cutting down on their outing. She also explained to Harinder that parents are adults. They can do certain activities as they know their limits and are financially independent. By lying to them he may get into wrong habits and doing things that are age inappropriate for him. Parents need better communication to know about his needs and feelings while he is alone, as it will be helpful in developing respect for each other.

Defying rules, lying and run away behaviours are not accepted as normal in the society. These are dealt with either by punishing adolescents in different forms or by idealistic preaching that makes them feel guilty and thus they pull away further. This is not helpful as adolescent would repeat the same next time. Understanding the underlying needs of teens is important. It thus needs talking about the problem. Many times an adolescent is part of a certain group which puts pressure on him. One needs to know about these influences. The providing of alternative opportunities to have different friends and pastime activities can change the context for the adolescent.

Day Dreaming and Fantasy

Adolescents live off and on in a dream world of their own. They fantasize various situations and derive pleasure of fulfilling their unrealistic wishes in the process. Although it is quite a normal behaviour, it becomes problematic in some cases when one resorts to it excessively to escape from the required activities.

Himani has been an above average student so far. Her performance started falling on her entry to class XI. She came to the school counselor herself one day and said 'Ma'am I am worried that I will fail. I can not study. I want to study and do well in class/exams, but when I sit down to study I can not concentrate. My teachers have noticed it and are asking if there is something wrong with me. Why I am not there at work despite my physical presence in the class?'

The counselor began to explore the possible causes of her loss of interest in studies but found no plausible reason, except that when she sat to study, she was unable to focus her attention and she kept thinking of one hundred different things and mainly the boys. In further discussions Himani revealed that other girls in the class have boy friends and they tell her interesting stories about their relationships with them. She on the other hand has no opportunity to interact with friends. She pointed out that her parents were very conservative and they did not allow her to talk to boys or to go out to meet her friends in the evening. She felt comfortable in fantasizing her relationships with different boys and girls, even when she is in the class or sitting alone at home. The counselor advised her to do some physical exercise or play games in the evening and pursue some hobby. The parents were also advised to encourage her to develop healthy friendships and relationships with boys and girls. She encouraged her to write a personal diary to let out her feelings.

Adolescents fantasize many relationships and spend hours to the extent that they are not able to concentrate on the required activities. For example, an adolescent may say that I am the favourite of my parents and not my brother, whereas in reality it might be just the opposite. They may fantasize getting attention from a teacher they admire or getting various awards which they aspire to, but are unable to get in reality and thus tell such imaginary stories to their parents and others. Adolescents should not be scolded on knowing the reality. It is just a need that they are unable to fulfill in real life. If possible, opportunities may be provided to fulfill their need. Effort may be made to change their thinking towards more realistic and achievable goals.

Managing Sexuality

Adolescents need to be able to manage their sexuality urges and relate to persons of opposite sex in a healthy manner. This does not happen in many cases because the family fails to reinforce in them the value of respecting the person of other sex. This happens more in case of boys than girls, resulting in instances of eve teasing and indecent behaviour.

Eve Teasing. It happens mostly to teenage and young college girls.

Kiran a student of class VIII came to the school counselor hesitatingly. 'Ma'am, I want to discuss something with you. I hope you will not tell anybody.' The counselor encouraged her to reveal her concerns. She said that while coming to the school on the public bus, a boy often comes and sits next to her. He keeps on shifting closer to her in a way that his body touches hers. She keeps moving aside but he keeps on shifting further. One day he also tried to pinch her at the thigh. She said 'I feel very uncomfortable. I have tried to remove his hand from my body several times. I feel if I will say anything to him or raise my voice others in the bus will come to know and will think ill of me. They may even make fun of me.' She added that she was very scared but does not know what to do? After a few days again when she was standing in the crowded bus the boy came and stood behind her and started rubbing against her. She said 'I really do not like it but do not know what to do. There are other boys who keep falling on us too. She has not shared it with her parents as she is afraid they will only scold her. She shared it with some of her close friends who told her not to discuss this with anybody.' The girl had no information about sexual urges in males. She had a guilt feeling as if she was encouraging such advances. She said she hates her body being touched. She feels dirty but helpless.

The counselor asked her not to be afraid and to deal with such situations confidently. She has right over her body. If anybody touches it she should tell the person firmly to stay away from her. She could take help of other females present on the situation. It will be better to go in the bus with her friends. She should also take her parents into confidence. Boys tend to fulfill their sexual needs in unhealthy manner in the absence of more positive outlets to meet the girls. However, some girls also find it a way of getting attention from boys. They should abstain from giggling or paying undue attention to boys. Girls need to be empowered to deal with such situations.

Indecent Behaviour. It may be displayed by an adolescent having highly permissive parents. An action negative and unpleasant to the eye cannot be ignored in school, however. Such adolescents irrespective of their predisposition need attention and if necessary, professional help.

There are cases of various adolescents indulging in obscene behaviours, like intentional rubbing of genitals and showing obscene pictures to others to exert their power over others. The underlying need is to rebel against the society who does not accept them. They have not been understood and are suppressed by their parents, teachers and other adults.

Depression/Suicidal Behaviour

Adolescents outnumber adults every year in cases of suicide. Two prominent causes of suicide among adolescents are frustrating love relationships and failure in examinations. Adolescents like to make friends of the same sex as well as of opposite sex as they find it easy to communicate and relate to them than parents. They are, however, not always successful because they have not acquired the necessary social skills to develop healthy peer relations, particularly with the opposite sex and face parental disapproval. More adolescent girls than boys find it stressful to build and carry on with friendships and they increasingly face relational aggression. More girls report going through periods of distress because their friends spread rumors about them and parents refuse to accept their explanations. It puts the adolescents involved at the receiving end. Some may be successful in getting away. Some fail and become trapped in their situation, making them feel compelled to end their life.

Stuti was studying in her room for her terminal exam in history the next day. The phone rang. After little conversation with her friend, she came running to her mother 'Ma, Ma Vaishali has taken Phenyl. She is half drowsy and is vomiting. It's about that boy she had confrontation with her mother. Ma, she may die. I should go to her house. Tell me what should I do? I am very worried for her.' Stuti's mother happened to be a Child Psychologist. She told her not to get worried about her friend. Instead, she will take care of her friend. She should relax. Realizing the gravity of the situation the mother rang up Vaishali's mother. She was taken to hospital and medical help was given.

Vaishali comes from an upper middle class family. She has a joint family with her grand parents living in the same house. The home provided a loving atmosphere. She was a student of class XI in a public school in Delhi, doing fairly well in her studies. She also took interest in other school activities. She had an elder brother so her parents did not mind her meeting the brother's friends. They were fairly open minded. She became friendly with a boy living in the neighbourhood. He was also her elder brother's friend. He was a Chinese but she started seeing him off and on. Her parents noticed their developing friendship, but thought it to be confined to platonic level which will finish with time. Gradually, they started becoming more emotionally involved with each other and spending more time together. Her parents started objecting to the friendship as her studies were getting adversely affected. As she had become very close to the boy, she even started lying to her parents in order to meet him. Many times she would not board the school bus and the boy would bring his father's car to drop her to the school. They thus, extended the time to be together. Once or twice she missed the school and spent the day roaming around with him. In the evenings under one pretext or the other she would slip out of the house to meet him. Her parents started becoming stricter with her and kept a close eye on her activities. Parents told her that she was too young to make any promises to any boy and that too with one of Chinese origin. They tried to reason out with her but would end in arguments.

Stuti's mother called Vaishali, empathized with her and showed an understanding of her situation and what she was facing. She suggested that no discussion can be done at this moment as she had lost control over herself. Effort was made to help Vaishali analyze her feelings towards her parents. After a long discussion she agreed that she cares for her parents' feelings and will not repeat her behaviour. Stuti's mother informed Vaishali's mother that her daughter needs immediate medical help, and her support and understanding. This issue can be talked about after the exams. Physically she should be with the girl most of the time and give her moral support. The mother was also assured that such things can happen with adolescents. Vaishali's mother followed the advice. After her exams the matter was discussed with parents and Vaishali together. Vaishali was told that in future she will not hide anything from parents. She was also made to understand that at this time she should pay more attention to her studies and a career for herself. Once she has a career, then only she should think of marriage.

Two other girls Malini and Pallavi students of class XII appeared in maths paper of the Board. Both felt they have not done well. Next they went home and committed suicide. Malini hanged herself using the scarf on the ceiling fan and leaving a note behind. Pallavi consumed poison and just slept and left no note behind. Both left the parents and teachers bewildered. In these cases the obvious cause was the failure to meet the expectations of self and/or others. Failing in exams need not be seen as the end of the world. Those not doing well in studies can appear in exams through correspondence courses and/or take vocational courses, once they are given emotional support to come out of the initial stress.

It is better to deal with the problem at an early stage rather than letting it build up resulting in a crisis situation. Adolescents may also get into situation of suicide and depression because of other causes, such as poor body image, loss of a loved one, demand for independence, peer rejection, pregnancy, low self-esteem etc. Parents and teachers should read early symptoms of depression and give them opportunity to express their concerns without derogating. School counselors may use appropriate psychometric methods to identify the areas of concern. For an adolescent about to commit suicide self-preservation becomes most important and one is not able to think of the consequences. One way to deal with the situation is to remind the adolescents of their loved ones. Comforting the person and high emotional support should be offered. Making the person talk about the concerns should be followed by counseling to avoid the recurrences.

Attitudes and Moods

Though persons in all age groups have specific attitudes with which they act and react to different issues/problems they confront in daily lives, no other age group enjoys the luxury of attitudes like teenagers. The attitude issue emerges to the fore as a prominent correlate of identity search during adolescence. Once the 'I' and 'Me' feelings become central to relationships with parents, peers and others, what an adolescent thinks gets reflected in attitudes towards them. Most parents of teenagers encounter attitude problems as a routine related to almost everything they ask them to do, from personal care to food, relationships, clothes and use of gadgets. The parents are irritated and troubled in the process of managing positive communication with them.

Adolescents' moods swing from one end to the other like the light switch being turned off and on. A minute feeling euphoric and another minute feeling despondent, truly characterize the mood swings of adolescents. Most times moodiness begins from things going in the minds of adolescents or a desire for privacy to concentration on oneself. Adolescents are not any more highly emotional than children and adults, except that they react strongly to both positive and negative events.

Prabha is 16 years old, pretty and well built. She is a student of class XI in a good school. She is an average student and is not interested in any activity in particular. Some days she is very well behaved and caring of parents and siblings, but very demanding and uncompromising on other days. Some days she is very happy with her work and life and some days, she just cries and is in bad temper for hours with everyone. She is very friendly with her classmates on some days and totally indifferent many other times. She has thus frequent tiffs with parents at home and with peer group. Her parents have consulted her doctor but no medical condition has been identified. She is going through hormonal changes, some of which she is having trouble in adapting to. She has been referred to the school counselor.

The school counselor working with Prabha felt that she expects too much from others at home and school without doing her part. She gets in an exalted mood when she gets what she wants and shows bad temper and attitude when she does not. She has not learnt that give and take is needed every day in all life situations. She was made to think of the ways she has been using to deal with others in various situations and their reactions towards her. She was also made to analyze her behaviour and expectations of others. Help was given to her to develop awareness of her duties, reciprocating to others and be sensitive to the needs of others at home. Parents were asked to encourage and reinforce the skills of empathy, patience and coping with emotions.

It may be difficult to deal with tempers and attitudes of teens every day. For parents the patience is the keyword. These will pass off with time. Do not react to their provocative attitudes as it further gives them the opportunity to showoff. Certain behaviours may be ignored. A loving but firm handling is definitely needed to encourage better adjustment. A habit of sharing responsibilities may be inculcated from the beginning. Parents must share their own limitations and concerns with adolescents.

Rebelling/Butting Heads

Rebellion in teenagers against parents is understood as a way of attempting to question and do away with the parental authority and control, and make themselves the master of own life. As teens mature they form their moral code, and parents consider it rebelling against their control. They take it as the teenager's rejection of parental values and beliefs. There are only some in reality who may be rebellious. Some common causes of teenage rebellion are—boyfriends/girlfriends; peer influence and pressure; popular music, movies and TV; less parental influence; and indifference to significant issues etc.

Tina is 15 years old and makes constant demand on parents for money. Mother (Rano) has given so far whatever asked for, but has begun to feel the heat. She is frustrated and fails to understand why her daughter needs money every day for something or the other, when she has been given everything by parents. If Tina does not get what she wants she throws herself into temper tantrums, gets louder, slams the doors and threatens to go away. What angers Rano the most is that Tina has no value of money and spends it in a mindless manner? Her brother Pallav does the same thing. Both the parents were so busy that they never discussed the money spending habits with kids and found escape in giving it right away. Since Tina is in her teens, if refused, she rebels more strongly. There are constant arguments between mother and daughter. Rano visited a counselor who told her that she and her husband should involve the growing up kids in the financial planning of the family. The counselor pointed out to her the value of introducing some discipline on money planning and saving for future from early years. Even if you don't want to give real numbers, you can discuss the plan, expenditure on school, annual vacation, household etc. They should also encourage them to do some saving out of their pocket money.

In the above case, better communication between the parents and adolescent during the period of growing up would help in better understanding of each others' needs and views and develop healthy moral codes.

Unplanned Attacks

Atul and Salman had been classmates since they were in class V. They are in class VIII now in a private school. They live in the same area and travel on the same school bus. While Salman has been a talkative boy he can use abusive language once provoked. Atul is friendly but somewhat closed and within his shell most of the times. He mixes only with a few boys and easily gets into fights even with them, if he does not like what they have said or done. He has a younger sister, whom he loves a lot but he does not share anything with her. He has hit her hard on some occasions. Parents often punish him but he cannot deal with his anger positively. Once provoked, he even hits children in neighbourhood and school. He plays cricket in school but remains highly self-focused. His parents and teachers often worry about his behaviour. One day while traveling on bus in the morning, his friends were discussing the last night match between India and Australia. Atul being a player had been picking on fine points and lapses of players. Salman did not like his comments but said nothing. They reached the school without finishing the discussion. They remained quiet on the bus back home and also on the bus to the school next day. On the bus home on the second day, they again got into arguments. As the two were nearing their bus stop to get down Atul hit Salman hard on his head with his cricket bat. Salman fell unconscious and was bleeding. The teachers on the bus took Salman to the hospital, where he got a few stitches and regained consciousness. The school suspended Atul for two days and the principal asked the parents for a meeting. When Atul returned to the school he was referred to the school counselor.

The counselor talked to Atul and asked for parents to meet her. She met the parents to find out if Atul was that aggressive at home with siblings or with children in the neighbourhood. Parents informed the counselor that Atul had been a well-behaved boy till about two years ago, when they noticed some changes in his behaviour, like bad temperament and sudden aggression. He does not talk much to family members and watches TV mainly other than his studies. One day he did get very angry with his sister and hit her hard. Parents considered this one odd act, talked to him and made him apologize to his sister. Things have been quite normal so far till this complaint. The counselor explained that adolescence brings in many changes and perhaps Atul once provoked finds it difficult to handle his emotions. He has a very high need to express himself. He seeks attention by doing such things. The counselor talked to Atul a few times and felt that he, needs help in developing the skill to deal with anger. Some tips on anger management were given. He injured Salman at the spur of moment and was very sorry for it. Parents should spend time with him. He has not internalized the basic values of patience, care and tolerance, and an all out effort needs to be made to help him in this task.

Road Rage

Road rage has become quite a serious behavioural issue in recent years among late adolescents. They are taking to the wheel and driving bikes and cars violating at times traffic rules or hit the other vehicles and then show muscle power. There have been days when more than one case of road rage occurred in a metro like Delhi.

Harinder (19 years), Kishan (19 years), Suniel (18 years), and Mrinal (16 years) were driving out of a pub on a Sunday night at 2.00 a.m. Harinder was in the driver seat and Suniel was sitting next to him in the passenger seat. Kishan and Mrinal were in the back seats. Two traffic cops on their bike noticed that Harinder was driving against the traffic flow. They signaled him to stop but he instead drove away at a record high speed. The cops chased the offender and forced him to stop. Harinder opened his window and abused the cops and then got into a scuffle with them. The traffic cop overpowered him but soon the other three joined the fight and thrashed the cop so badly that he had to be admitted in a hospital. They also tore their challan book and tried to snatch the revolver of the head constable. On examination it was found that all the occupants had alcohol and Harinder tested significantly higher than permissible limit. As Mrinal was still in the school it made news in the media. This embarrassed the school authorities. Next day, he was pulled up by the principal and his parents were called for a meeting. It came out that parents had no knowledge about the habits and whereabouts of their ward. Whenever they tried to know, he just ignored and walked out. They were asked by the principal to maintain a close watch on Mrinal's outings as he was not doing academically well either, and had been involved in some fights at the school. They were also requested to take some professional help as he was not old enough to be smoking and drinking at pubs. In another case Ankur (17 years) went out with classmates to a party. They all drank there. While coming back he failed to brake the car at the police barrier and ran on the footpath crushing a labourer who was sleeping there and fell into the legal tussle. He was driving without a license, which reflected negatively on the mind set of parents.

Parents should set some limits for adolescents alongwith giving the privileges. These days with the availability of numerous electronics items for growing teens and every parent wanting to provide the best to their ward, it has become necessary to guide the teens in the judicious use of items. Respect for law and social rules should be encouraged rather than praise for defying them and taking law in their own hands.

Bullying

Bullying during adolescence is common and can take many forms: physical, emotional, verbal or a combination of these. It may involve one person bullying another, a group of youngsters against a single person, or groups against other groups (gangs). It may involve girls as well as boys. The big bully takes perverse pleasure in tormenting others and the frightened and cowered few resent it yet take it.

Akhilesh, Navin, and Manish have just moved to a suburb of the metro city with their parents and have been admitted to class VIII in a very elite school. Akhilesh's father is a businessman of good standing. He has been a college graduate and mother has finished senior secondary school. Navin and Manish have fathers who did not finish college and are neo riches after disposing their agricultural land to a builder. They have plenty of parental money and property and are living off a lavish life. Navin's father has a licensed revolver and has taught Navin how to use it. They both in fact, boast about it and try to impress everyone how good a social status the revolver gives them. Navin and Manish are close friends and do things for each other even if wrong. Akhilesh had talked to them provokingly sometime in the past in the school. They both felt angry and reported to the parents and teachers. Parents kept quiet and waited for the teacher to act. Teacher ignored it completely. Akhilesh seemingly abused Navin again and pushed him. Navin felt very hurt. He talked to Manish that they should do something about it. Next morning, Navin took out the father's revolver and hid it in his socks. On reaching school he transferred it to his school bag. He took Manish aside and told him that after the school they will call Akhilesh to the corridor and when he is alone, they will jointly shoot him. After the classes were done and other children went into bus lines, they called Akhilesh to the side corridor. First Navin fired two shots and then Manish fired one shot killing Akhilesh. This made headline in the media and became a police case, in which even fathers of Navin and Manish were arrested. The debate among public, teachers and counselors kept on going in the media that why have the parents and teachers ignored the earlier cues. Akhilesh's parents had to go through regular counseling to help them come out of the trauma, which they may never grow out completely. To them Akhilesh never was sort of bully, rather he had been subjected to jokes and abuses many times and school did nothing even after complaining.

Bullies are apparently students who have been bullied or abused themselves at home or at school. They do not fit in the group and are not able to meet the expectations of their family or school. They bully to feel competent, successful, control someone else, and to get some relief from their own feelings of powerlessness. The bullies and victims both have low self-esteem and lack social skills. Victims feel insecure, fail to pick up social cues, become emotionally distraught easily and are unable to defend or stand up for themselves. Some teens may tease bullies and make themselves a target by egging the people on, not knowing when to stop, and then not being able to effectively defend themselves when the balance of power shifts to the bully. Teens who are not bullied have better social and conflict management skills. They can assert themselves about differences without being aggressive or confronting. They are more aware of people's feelings and are the ones who can be helpful in resolving disputes.

The school authorities, psychiatrists and psychologists have expressed their concern about increased instances of bullying, and violence among teenagers. Teens are perhaps learning a lot of it in their social context from TV, video, games on the net which use violence as the medium of entertainment. These may act as the triggers for some teens. Anger is a natural emotion and children need to learn ways of handling it beginning at home to school and community. When neither home nor school addresses the problem, it does erupt in a serious form. Sometimes the child gets mixed signal at home, like parents talking at dinner table 'you should not take things without showing your feelings'. All teens need to be sensitized to the pain of others. Bully's dignity should not be undermined. They need to be understood, thus the necessity of communication and empathy. Confront them and make it clear that their behaviour is not acceptable. Some training into life skills may be desirable for all.

In schools the approach must be comprehensive and ongoing to effectively address adolescents' social needs, like,

(1) creating a climate of safety and respect for each other; (2) teaching social skills to all; and (3) defining predictable expectations and implementing consistent behaviour. When negative behaviours are tolerated and not addressed appropriately, kids may feel scared or socially isolated. Inculcating a sense of pride in one's actions and intentions may help teens to behave responsibly and with others in mind. One has to be vigilant for cues, because if left unattended the bullying may continue for longer and have more difficult consequences for the adolescent and the family as seems to have happened in case of Akhilesh.

Parents should encourage the teens to speak out, stay in groups and inculcate resilience in them. The common methods of handling it, like classroom discussions, role playing and detentions are not much effective. Adolescents live in a social culture where the norms and expectations are overwhelmingly present, yet are not always clearly defined. The struggle for power and status is a strong motivator in friendships. Teens need an open forum and a context where they can feel empowered to interact respectfully and develop healthy relationships.

Role of Parents and Teachers

There are many adolescents bordering on the side of behavioural issues. They need the help of parents and teachers. Some suggestions are given here:

1. Have Friendly Interactions. Parents and teachers should interact with teens more as friends than in positions of authority. They should regularly communicate with them and interchange ideas how and where to use their growing energy in a productive manner. They should listen patiently to what they say and try to understand the underlying causes that bother them.

2. Early Note of Cues. Read signals early and in case of a problem do not push it under the carpet. Remember that no negative behaviour is acquired over night; it is only that you did not notice it. Or you waited to let the good sense of the teen prevail. Once noticed in any form, try to make the adolescent feel comfortable and encourage talking to find out the underlying cause. Show sensitivity to the underlying needs. Accept the inadequacies, reassure and make the adolescent explore the possibilities and alternatives. Help her/him to regain the lost confidence.

3. Allow Them to Talk. Many of the troubles start when adolescents are not able to express themselves. Opportunities should be given for self-expression in the form of writing a personal diary or drawing or acting out in addition to talking in an atmosphere of warmth and understanding. Help them to develop good communication skills.

4. Help to Redefine Goals. An adolescent in trouble needs help in redefining personal goals, what s/he wanted to achieve and what significant others expect. Allow them to express their dreams. Provide opportunities for exploring and pursuing alternatives.

5. Respect Uniqueness. Instead of comparing the adolescent with others you know, encourage and accept the difference. Convey this honestly to the adolescent to make her/him proud about what one is.

6. Teach Positive Values. Spend time with your teens and inculcate values of fairness, respect, patience, and tolerance for differences. They should learn from early years the virtues of honesty, telling truth, not to look down at persons lower in status, love and care for humanity, and have compassion.

7. Adhere to Rules. Set rules that can be followed and be firm. Do not change them often and without discussing with the adolescent. Monitor their time and activity schedule.

8. Give Space. Allow reasonable amount of time and freedom to meet their friends and have some privacy. Give responsibilities to match their abilities and increase them gradually but do not over burden. Build a relationship of mutual trust.

9. Help to Develop Problem Solving Skills. Give your ward some training in developing the habit of weighing the pros and cons on their own and to resolve the problems.

10. Watch for Comfort Levels. Many young people with low achievement level can do well in life. Teachers should make them feel comfortable and accepted in the classroom.

11. Give Sense of Belonging. It is important to make them feel that irrespective of anything they do, they will always have their parents and place to return waiting for them. Parents will always be there for them. Parents should opt for proactive strategies and be willing to change them depending on the situations.

12. Accept Help. Encourage them to talk to the school counselor periodically, even if there is no problem. Do not shy away from taking your teen to the school counselor or for professional help, if needed.

10

Smoking and Drugs

Example is not the main thing in influencing others, it is the only thing.

Albert Schweitzer

Concerns Voiced

'We are very worried about our son if he is smoking or drinks with his friends without telling us' said the parent of a 15 years old to the school counselor while seeking her professional advice during a PTA meeting. It is a real problem, admitted the counselor. She said that technically the selling of tobacco products, alcohol or other drugs to persons below 18 years in age is a legal offense. Yet instances abound of adolescents buying and consuming cigarettes, alcohol and other drugs like, brown sugar, cocaine and marijuana. The consumption of these products shows an upward trend among adolescents, despite the fact that it puts them at risk for variety of health and cognitive problems, such as, problems affecting lungs and immune system, heart attacks, depression, difficulty in concentration, poor grades, criminal activities, and risky sexual behaviours.

Smoking

Adolescents' may consume tobacco in the form of smoking cigarette/bidi/clover. It is observed that those who begin to smoke as adolescents have a higher probability of becoming adult smokers. Cigarette advertisements emphasize themes of youthful vigour, sexual attraction and independence, which are quite appealing to teenagers and young adults.

Sulabh is a student of class VI in a private school. He is 12 years old. Both of his parents work, and he has a servant at home to look after him on his return from school. The servant is young and smokes bidis. Sulabh has been watching him for a couple of years and now finds it difficult to resist the temptation. One day he asked the servant to give him his bidi. First he did not like it, but in a few days he felt like taking it even if he did not like and then got used to it. He talked to a close friend and found that he has not done anything wrong. Many other boys are into smoking cigarettes off and on. He thus graduated to cigarettes. First, he was smoking outside but now he smokes in his room. One day when his mother came in to organize his room, she smelled smoking. Parents then confronted Sulabh. He admitted that he is smoking and that his other friends are also doing it. Parents talked to him. The school counselor also talked about the dangers of smoking to the class. It was tough but for now Sulabh stopped smoking. Early detection helped Sulabh against smoking to form into a habit. Yellow brown marks on the nails and fingers tips are the other signs of smoking for parents to watch and be on alert. Often school-going adolescents are afraid of being caught, and thus they hide cigarettes either in their own or in friends' school bags/cupboards. Initially one may take one or two puffs out of curiosity to see how it feels and then may get swayed.

Adolescents having parents or friends smoke are more prone to smoking, while those having a positive view of school, religious involvement, or conventional type friends are much less inclined to smoke. Parents often feel powerless to restrain their ward against it when they find other teens indulging in the same practice. They are afraid that even if they try hard they may end up having their ward socially isolated or smoking behind their back. They should maintain good communication with their growing teens to be able to successfully restrain them. Smoking is found strongly associated with other teenage problem behaviours, such as, delinquency, problem drinking, marijuana use, and pre-marital sex relationships.

Alcohol and Drugs

Veena, Ashima, Kavita and Bini of class X in a renowned public school were very close friends. On midway in class X they felt that now they were close to being 16 years and quite grown up to do whatever they find interesting. In between the classes or whenever a teacher was absent, they began to sneak out to the games field. Gradually as the year progressed, their frequency of coming out of the class increased and many times they were not even noticed. They found a raised platform behind the lush green bushes as a very convenient place to sit and laze around. This became their favourite place to while away their time. They heard their seniors telling each other- 'Let's have a fag. Life is too boring.' They adopted this as one of their favourite phrases too. Once there, Veena would take out cigarettes from her school bag and share puffs with Ashima and Kavita. Bini was in the same group and a favourite of all, but she somehow refrained from smoking. Sometimes after school when there were extra classes and they did not have to board the school bus, they would walk down to the corner shop and buy three cigarettes. They did not want to keep extras with them lest parents may notice it. Ashima and Kavita were afraid of being caught by their parents, whereas Veena did not bother as her parents never came to her room. These girls had become very close pals. After the class X Board exams finished, they would go out together to different places and have fun. During whole of summer vacation they shared many adventures and new experiences. They also had sleepovers at each other's place. When their Board results came, they all had done reasonably well. To celebrate their success they got together at Veena's house. They purchased a bottle of scotch and brought it home. After parents went to sleep, they went outside to sit in the balcony near the bedroom and each shared a peg. They felt quite thrilled by the new experience. They kept on repeating this practice whenever they spent the night together at anyone's house. Veena would generally have more than one peg. They also started visiting pubs by the end of class XII. There they would drink, dance and have fun. Veena's drinking frequency increased over time. She would often return home quite drunk as she knew her parents will not be there, whereas for others it remained an occasional event. Bini who refrained from taking cigarettes and liquor even in class XI, became familiar with the names of various types of liquor, from mild to the hard ones. In class XII she tasted Bacardi, rationalizing that it contained very little percent of alcohol and had more of juice.

After passing the class XII Boards, these girls alongwith two other girls went to Kullu Manali on a trip with the consent of their parents. On coming back Bini, who was very open with her parents, narrated all her experiences to them. Besides telling about various adventures, she told them that 'one evening we bought a bottle of whiskey and six of us had it. Even I took one peg. Nothing happened to me. But two other girls became totally drunk. I did not like it and I think I will never have it again.' Parents though taken aback respected her confession as well as the decision not to repeat drinking. Veena, Ashima and Kavita continued to have drinks occasionally during their college years. Bini drank Bacardi few more times, but later stopped it altogether. At college Veena indulged even in other drugs and smoked pot. She did not become a habitual but continued to smoke pot off and on. She felt that it gave her a euphoric feeling. Her friendship now extended to a group in which drug taking was considered hap.

All these girls had started smoking first to kill their boredom by imitating what the seniors were doing. They considered smoking and drinking an in-thing. They could not think what was right and what was wrong. To them it showed style. The sudden freedom and opportunities to move around gave them chance to try out many new experiences/behaviours. Adolescents are very impressionable at their age. They start doing many things under the influence of others. In Veena's case, parents did not have time. Her parents did not have much interaction with her. Many times she would hide things from them and did what she wanted to do. She took to drugs as a temporary escape/relief from being alone.

Similar to these girls there are many adolescents who indulge in occasional smoking and drinking to try out new experiences/things. They consider it as a done thing in an adult role. Adolescents take it as a time pass to escape the boredom or when there is no other constructive pas-time activity. The adolescence is characterized as an age vulnerable to peer pressure and group activities. They find drug use fitting the bill as it takes place generally in the company of peers. Media also focuses on teens' smoking and using drugs to portray style and trends in industry and society.

There are many adolescents like Bini who get carried away under peer pressure just to try out a new behaviour as others are doing, but consciously control themselves and abstain. After trying out the drugs a couple of times they are able to make a right judgment for themselves. Some seeing others may say 'No' right in the beginning. These adolescents demonstrate that they have developed right values from the childhood, and parents have open communication with them who continue to guide them in the chosen direction. Their decision-making is based on reasoning. They value parent's views and parents value their opinions. Further, parents remain their role models, as seen in case of Bini who had not seen her parents drinking liquor as a matter of habit. Her father took one or two drinks at parties only. Other girls had seen liquor being used by parents most evenings and abundantly served in their homes during parties. Thus these girls had few inhibitions in starting to drink. The behaviour of the above girls also emphasized the need of reducing the study pressure on students. Often students shuffle from one class to another without having any time in between to breathe/soothe their nerves. There are times when students want to completely block the routine experiences by resorting to drug use.

It is seen as a major change that a good number of the teenage girls are indulging in smoking and drinking. They have no inhibitions in going to a liquor shop. Perhaps they are emboldened by the social changes. Earlier youth would indulge in such behaviour only when they started earning or were at college, but now many school-going teenagers drink and smoke. It has been argued that it happened more now because of the reduced parent-child communication time, lack of adherence to moral values, and parents not portraying correct ideal image to their wards.

A Class Teacher Worked on a Case of Drug Use

This case of alcohol use involved a group of eight students of class XI in the Commerce stream. All of them had an excellent rapport with their Economics teacher Mrs. Maitri, who was also their class teacher. Students would generally confide in her for personal problems. As a result she was always surrounded by students. One day while Mrs. Maitri was sitting in her room correcting copies, one student named Dilip was going up and down outside her room trying to attract her attention. Dilip had a sigh of relief when she asked him if he had something to talk to her. He made a gesture with his hand requesting her to come out as there were two more teachers sitting with her. On coming out she asked him what did he want to share with her. Dilip replied 'Ma'am but we cannot talk here. Can we go to some other place where nobody would notice us? They looked for a little secluded place in the school and settled there?

Dilip started 'Ma'am the group of eight boys and girls that had gone for a school trip to Goa, have been planning for the last few days to have beer party after school hours. Today finally they have brought beer to the school, which they are going to have in the classroom after the school finishes. There is lot of excitement about this among the students. Nobody is concentrating on studies. Ma'am please do not cite my name. The whole class will get very angry with me. But I really think it is wrong and that my classmates should not be indulging in it.' The class had good deal of solidarity.

Mrs. Maitri was very fond of her class. As she had developed lot of faith in them she felt quite let down and felt really shattered on hearing the news. She went to her room and sat alone for some time to deal with her feelings. She realized that something has to be done about it quickly to nip the bud now, lest others may follow this example. She explored various possibilities of handling the situation. It occurred to her that she should call these students and confront them directly. She also thought of taking it to the Principal but felt that punitive methods were not going to help. She felt that sharing the information with other staff members may become a scandal. Finally, she picked up her cell and rang up the school counselor to advise her about handling the whole affair. Together, they decided not to adopt punitive ways as these will not be of much help in the long run. Rather they should talk to the students. The students were called to the school counselor's room. As Mrs. Maitri had great rapport with the class, she straight away asked these students about what she had heard. First, they tried to deny the whole issue. 'Ma'am it is not like this.' But when she threatened that she will have to inform the Principal about it as she is responsible for discipline of her class, they admitted that Abhinav has bought beer and brought it to the school. They have developed a strong bond ever since they had gone on the school trip, and have been making several programmes together. When she asked them why they planned such a thing, they said they were still in an adventurous mood and wanted to have this thrill. They have heard so much about others taking to drinks and in the media. It also came to the notice of Mrs. Maitri that liquor was used regularly in the homes of some of the students. They were thus interested in trying it out. The students were reminded of the school discipline and the importance of abiding by the school norms. The teacher explained to them about other healthy and novel ways of having excitement and thrill, such as going out for sight seeing, having a dance and music party at some person's place, going and helping in some institution, viewing some exhibition etc. They were explained the harmful effects of liquor consumption and how unintentionally it leads to habit formation and addiction. It adversely affects the body processes and effective functioning of a person via its effects on the central nervous system. Mrs. Maitri informed the Principal about the event and also about how she tackled the whole issue. The Principal was quite sensitive to the adolescent issues. She came forward to talk to these students personally so that they would realize the gravity of the problem but did not use any punitive methods. It was felt necessary to bring the issue to the notice of parents, so that care could be taken even at home.

The class teacher also discussed in the class the effects of using liquor, without mentioning the eight students.

It was observed in the above case that the adolescents were unaware of the ill-effects of alcohol. They wanted to try out new things for enjoyment and have some thrill by consuming alcohol, as they see in the society and media that people have alcohol for enjoyment. During adolescence taking of alcohol starts as a group adventure, although all adolescents do not resort to it. Certain students having solid values are able to say 'no'. This case highlights the teachers' role in the decision making of students, to help them think seriously prior to taking alcohol. The teacher's personal rapport and communication prevented the onset of an addictive habit. No punitive methods or controls can help in reality. Rather a loving but firm attitude to help students should be adopted. During adolescence norms of behaviour should be laid down clearly. The harmful effects of taking alcohol and getting addicted should be explained to them periodically. Teachers and parents should emphasize alternative modes of entertainment.

An Ex-Student Recollected Experiences of Last Two Years in School

An ex-student recalled that in the last two years of the school (classes XI & XII) he and some of his friends used to take drugs. 'Initially, I took to drugs to experiment with it and have fun. Since others were taking it, they kept on pushing me repeatedly to try it and one day almost forced me to have it. Initially, I had some reservations telling myself that I should not be taking drugs as it is not considered a good practice. Also, if I get caught by elders what will they think about me. After lot of confusion and conflict in my mind, I gave in and decided to try since so many others in my group were taking it. Thus, I smoked the pot with my friends to show that I could take it and prove my masculinity. We would smoke pot sitting in the school toilets. This made our visits to the school toilets quite frequent. We would get scolded by the PT Sir that why there was so much noise in the school toilets. We would tell each other that the 'panther' is coming hush! hush! and we would let him pass. It remained unnoticed to the teachers. The drug powder was available with the pan shop at the corner. One of us would purchase it from the shop after school. We even started taking it to friends' places, where generally we would know that the parents were not there. We would spend long time in the evenings at their place. On coming home I would go straight into my room and would often miss the dinners pretending I was not hungry as I had something outside. My habit of taking drugs increased. By the end of class XII, I even started taking it in my own house, whenever parents were away or when they were asleep. A cinema complex was also our favourite hang out with friends. We would even have it there as it was sold there. I became somewhat careless in my studies. I reduced my participation in extra-curricular activities in school. All the time all of us in the group would be thinking of taking the next smoke. My parents noticed some changes in my behaviour. I kept on making false excuses by attributing it to the pressure of being in the higher class. Gradually I learnt to tell clean lies. Coming to class XII, I began to consume the drug in large dozes. I kept telling my parents I was not well. They could not pay much attention to me as they were going through some family chaos during that period. Once or twice they complained of toilets smelling of the drugs, but I pretended I didn't know anything. I think I had killed my conscience.'

'My school performance consistently declined from getting distinctions in class X to have become an average student. I kept telling myself that I will do better next time, till the December term exams when I managed to get just the passing marks. I got a warning from the school that if I do not improve in the pre-Boards I will not be allowed to sit in the finals. This gave me a tremendous shock as I had never got such low marks. I promised to myself that I will do better in the pre-Boards. I encountered difficulty in concentrating on studies. I had missed out so much that I had no courage to make up. Again one call from my friends and I would be there with them like a subservient to them and smoking again. I was not able to resist the temptation. I tried my best to at least sit down to study for some more hours, which I started doing for some days, but could not resist going to the farewell party organized for the class or other parties in the group. The farewell party was at a farm house. All the students of classes XII and XI were at the party. There was a DJ playing the popular songs. There was food and alcohol just like all other parties. My friends had come with enough supply of drugs for the night, and I could not miss out on it. So, we were all including girls, smoking-up, dancing and having a good time. I was introduced to a few new drugs there, like Acid, Ecstasy and Gum. The party lasted till 4.00 o'clock in the morning. There was free serving of drugs, from mild to the harsher ones, from expensive to non-expensive ones. As the night progressed, the inhibitions got loosened. There was lot of hugging and kissing going on between boys and girls. They started looking for more private places and had sex. The girls going back after 4.00 o'clock, in the morning had to make excuses at home that after 1.00 o'clock they spent the night at their friend's place, whereas boys took the advantage of being male in society. Next day, I stayed in the bed whole day because of the hangover. On this day I realized that what I was doing was completely wrong. I started to tell myself everyday to develop the courage to leave it someday. My father and a counselor worked with me. I finally succeeded in giving it up.'

'I am indeed thankful to my father who gave me his all out support during the two months before the exams. He would stay awake till 1.00 o'clock in the morning, reading books and watching TV, make me hot/cold drinks, talk to me, and go to bed only after I would finish my studies and go to bed. He was conscious of the fact that my performance was not like it used to be. He wanted to help me anyhow. Since evening he would be around, keep a watch on me, bring variety of eatables and joke in between to make me feel relaxed. I passed my class XII with fairly good marks, though not so good as to get admission on merit. By giving capitation fee my father got me admission in a private Law college. I am thankful to my father and feel sorry for my behaviour for putting heavy burden on him. I feel I was capable of much more. Why didn't I do my duty? My father assured me that I will do well now. I know and accept that I was wrong.'

There are many other boys and girls who consume drugs. They remain uncaught by teachers and parents, but they harm themselves and live with a guilty feeling throughout. 'I feel bad for Joy, my class fellow. He became an addict and could not leave the drugs. He would have withdrawal symptoms if he did not take. He had started taking it excessively, whereas some of us remained occasional users. He even started stealing money from his parents' drawers or borrowed from friends which he could never return. He could not appear for XII Boards and had to repeat the year. He had to be taken to drug de-addiction centre for treatment by professionals. He was given anti-addiction drugs, counseling and was placed later in a rehabilitation programme. I regret for my two years of school and would advice others to keep away from drugs.'

The above cited cases showed how a number of the adolescents fall into the drug trap by trying to experiment with various drugs. It is in general in the company of their peer group. Most of them remain unnoticed by their parents or teachers till they begin to show some visible symptoms. During this period there are some adverse effects in their normal functioning, such as neglect of studies, telling lies, becoming insensitive to their surroundings, stealing etc. Some may get even hooked to it and are unable to leave it. They may withdraw from society and have to undergo specialized treatment.

Why do Adolescents Resort to Drug Use

Adolescents may use drugs for many reasons, such as:

- **Peer Pressure.** Smoking and drug taking among adolescents starts generally under peer pressure. Some find it hard to resist the threat of social isolation, or to say 'no', or being left out. Being a part of the group gives them emotional strength and a 'we feeling', and they succumb to the pressure.

- **Academic Failure.** A teen who fails to tap into academic success as a source of self-esteem may try to dull the pain of the failure by using drugs. School related factors that increase the likelihood of such behaviour are: being held back a grade in school, low grade point average, early and persistent behavioural problems, low commitment to school, lack of peer acceptance in the elementary grades.

- **Little Knowledge of Harm Done.** Some do not understand the harmful effects of the use of substance. They have the mistaken belief that it will not lead to addiction.
- **Curiosity and Fun.** A good number of adolescents take drugs out of curiosity or for fun, thrill and adventure. They tryout a new adult behaviour and enjoy the euphoric feeling.
- **Lifestyle.** Some associate it with lifestyle as it connects them with their seniors, celebrities or do what media portrays.
- **Killing Boredom.** Some may begin to use it to kill boredom in the absence of healthy ways of passing time/recreation.
- **Easy Availability.** It is easily available outside the schools with the vendors, pan shops and in cinema complexes, the common hang out jaunts for adolescents.
- **Stress.** Adolescents who are under stress may fall easy prey to drugs as it offers to them an easy escape from the stress causing situation, although it may lead to addiction over time. The cause of stress may be pressure of studies, inability to meet the expectations of the parents or teachers, or inability to make appropriate career choice, unhappy home environment due to friction or separation between parents, parents' not giving time to children, or alcoholic parents.
- **Lack of Communication with Parents.** Some adolescents are not able to communicate with parents and are in constant conflict with them.
- **Low Self-esteem.** If an adolescent has low self-esteem one may resort to taking drugs to enhance the self-image or to relieve the underlying anxiety caused by low self-image.
- **Free Money.** If an adolescent gets too much free money one may be tempted to misuse it by experimenting with drugs.
- **Depression/Mood Swings.** There are some adolescents who feel depressed or already have trouble with their mood

swings and thus resort to taking alcohol or/and other drugs. All persons if not checked early run the risk of becoming addicted and may have more trouble getting off their addiction.

What Happens on Using Drugs

The consumption of tobacco, alcohol and other drugs can have a variety of harmful effects on the body and mind of users. It has physical, psychological, aspiration related and social consequences.

- **Physical Consequences.** The prolonged use of tobacco may cause respiratory problems, cardiovascular ailments and cancer of mouth and lungs. The use of alcohol adversely affects the central nervous system. Initially the person may feel relaxed, but slowly as the person becomes intoxicated the motor control is reduced and speech becomes unclear. The person's sensitivity to the surroundings becomes poorer. The use of substance leads to poor attention span and loss of memory. It also leads to weight loss and poor muscle toning. It reduces stamina and physical performance. Or conversely it causes overeating and weight gain.

- **Psychological Consequences.** In adolescents drug taking affects their ability to concentrate on studies. They feel lazy and not motivated to do any serious work. They have lower ability to focus and think clearly. They can "lose control" and make bad decisions. It sets in the feeling of helplessness and pessimism. It leads to behavioural changes and gradually to low self-esteem. Adolescents start telling lies and steal money to have more drugs.

Although elementary school-aged children vaguely know and accept the wide range of physical and psychological risks associated with drug use, it is in the secondary school that adolescents are more vulnerable to pro-use pressures. Again late adolescents (secondary school students) give little credence to the idea that substance use can cause them to suffer dire, irreversible damage.

- **Aspirational Consequences.** These may be short-term or long term, ranging in severity from minor inconveniences to major setbacks that can change the course of one's life (e.g., not getting into college). The short-term consequences may be such as losing some privileges, failing a test, getting thrown off a sports team, not having enough money for other activities, doing badly at school work, and having trouble with one's parents/teachers. The long-term consequences may be self-injury and dropping out of school. Many of these effects result from loss of motivation and deterioration in mental and physical capacities, while some may result because of adolescents' likelihood to make bad decisions and indulge in risky behaviours.

- **Social Consequences.** Drug taking can lead to socially unacceptable behaviours including unprotected sex. One may act in ways that make one look foolish and "uncool" (like hanging out with losers, or letting others take advantage of oneself). It can alienate one from friends. It makes parents angry and sad when they find their ward using cigarettes, drugs, marijuana etc. One can thus lose the trust and respect of parents and siblings; and have a negative influence on siblings. One's teachers will think low of the person and would not want him/her in the class as it would be bad influence on other students.

Do's for Parents & Teachers

1. **Recognize Individual Differences.** Recognize that different persons react to tobacco and drug taking differently. Some adolescents may smoke and take drinks for quite a while and yet not show problems. Others may have problems after the first use.

2. **Act Early.** The use of tobacco and drugs should be stopped at the earliest before it becomes a habit. Any change in normal behaviour of the adolescent may be viewed with sensitivity. If an adolescent is showing signs of hiding things from parents, makes unjustified demands for money, remains out unreasonably, remains drowsy or is not able to conduct himself normally, is rubbing in hands small rolled or burnt papers, these are indicative of smoking and/or drug use.

3. Communicate. Parents should keep communication channels open with their adolescents. Parents may talk to them about the use of tobacco and drugs and its harmful effects. They may be warned that with frequent use of tobacco and drugs a person is bound to move towards addiction or getting hooked to it forever.

4. Enable Them to say 'No'. As adolescents begin to use tobacco and drugs in the company of their peer group, they should be enabled to say 'No' to wrong things. Adolescents who are able to say 'No' should be recognized by the parents and the teachers for their right decision.

5. Encourage Sharing of Concerns and Seeking Support. Help may be given to them to develop healthy relations with friends, relatives, neighbours beyond immediate family on whom they can depend for support.

6. Help to Accept Failure and Distress. Success and failure are part of life. One may suffer setbacks from time to time. It may be seen as opportunity to grow. Other alternatives may be provided.

7. Find Alternative Sources of Fun. As adolescents begin to use drugs to have adventure and fun, emphasize to them alternative modes of recreation and entertainment. Adolescents enjoy listening to music. Dancing gives them an outlet for release of their energy and to be with friends. Other creative activities as painting, designing, craft, etc. may be encouraged. Outing, exhibitions, theatre, picnics, and excursions also give them fun and adventure.

8. Emphasis on Personal Growth. Put emphasis on self-control and personal growth. Tell them that refusal to accept peer pressure for tobacco and drugs indicates their personal strength. They can now assert their identity and are self-confident.

9. Negate 'Self-Positivity' Bias. The consequences of using tobacco and drugs are more severe now than in the past, because the drugs are more potent and the social and physical environment is more dangerous. Parents should not think that their ward will not take these under any circumstance.

10. Improve Parenting Skills. Strengthen your skills in areas of communication and family management. Be involved in and actively monitor the adolescents' activities. Establish rules that decrease the likelihood of the adolescents' being in situations that can lure them to tobacco and drug use. Build trust so that they keep you informed of their activities all the time. Encourage compliance with the rules and use only mild negative consequences for infractions.

11

Career Guidance

If you can dream it, you can do it.

Walt Disney

'A number of students of senior classes have been coming to me since they finished their first term to get information on courses and careers,' said Mrs. Chauhan the school counselor. 'Some want to know about the different courses they can do once they finish their X and/or XII Boards, some about the appropriate coaching classes, and some about available careers and how to make the appropriate choices.' Mrs. Chauhan talked to the principal about the need of setting some facility at school, that can provide information on changing career scenario to students on a regular basis and give some career guidance.

Career Scenario

The liberalization of economies coupled with complex scientific and technological developments of the last two decades or so has transformed the career scenario globally. It has thrown open new challenges and career options for the prospective candidates, while making obsolete many of the earlier career areas and job skills. The impact is found startling both at the institution and individual levels. The institutions are faced with the need to expand and renovate infrastructures, upgrade teacher skills and create new information systems for the variety of users (administrators, teachers, students and others). Teachers, parents and students are required to move away from stereotypical preferences of typical occupations and to consider and accept the values bundled in emerging career related courses and choices. The teachers, counselors and parents need to encourage and guide the youngsters in making career choices, in which they will do well and enjoy over the years. They also need to accept and inculcate in students the attitude that their first career choice may not be the lasting choice over work life. As suggested in the report of the International Commission on Higher Education (1996), the pace of development has made it inevitable that most youth may be changing their occupation 3-4 times in their work life, which means that they need constant openness and preparedness for upgrading their existing skills and training into new skills. The teachers, counselors and parents should be prepared to equip themselves with new information on an ongoing basis, lest they will not be able to help their wards in making appropriate course/career choices. They need to broaden their outlook and help the adolescents in a more informed and logical way to tackle the questions—what career to choose, what subjects are appropriate to study, what is most suitable for them keeping in view their personal and contextual predispositions, where the training facilities exist, what are the resource investments that are required to be made over time, and how to accomplish their goals? The task requires tremendous amount of planning, and information building to cater to the needs of multiple level users, and an equally powerful system of dissemination and delivery.

Career Development: Stages

Career development is a continuous process that evolves slowly through different stages of life. It gets shaped through a complex procedure in which many variables contribute interactively over a long period. Career is the most important aspect of human life and a part of healthy living. The type of career one will opt for will affect one's whole life. It becomes the source of everyday happiness or unhappiness for the person as well as the family and significant others in one's life. The career alone would determine the type of activities one will be routinely engaging in future to contribute to the well-being of self, family and society, what lifestyle one will have, where will one live, what type of people will one interact with and where will his achievements take him etc.? It thus necessitates that adolescents, parents, teachers and counselors treat it as important, invest their time and resources in understanding the person and the career, and undertake the necessary planning, information gathering and guidance.

The career of a person is affected by one's personal predispositions, the environment and other socio-cultural influences around her/him and the guidance available whenever needed. It requires lot of understanding about oneself-abilities, interests, aptitudes, personality traits, values and emotional state. It also requires information about the world of work and then matching the two. The more knowledge the adolescent acquires the better will be the career choice. Career choice is not a one point decision and takes place over a period of time. It depends on the interaction of individual with the environment and follows a pattern in development.

The career development process starts quite early in life and continues till late. Some of the distinct but overlapping stages of career development are mentioned below. From the perspective of adolescents only the second stage is of crucial importance:

0 to 14 years— a growth period.

14 to 25 years— a period of career exploration and choice.

25 to 45 years— a stage of stabilization.

45 to 65 years— a maintenance stage.

65 years— a stage of decline.

0-14 (A period of growth)—To begin with the child learns by observing persons around doing different types of jobs. As the child grows a little older s/he starts imitating them and plays roles of a doctor, teacher or banker etc. From these small beginnings one acquires some understanding of different types of activities people indulge in and keeps on building on these till one reaches middle school. During middle school as one comes in contact with the broader world, one's knowledge about various occupations gets enlarged. The person sees and hears about people working in different occupations and internalizes the relevant information. In school, the class on SUPW (Socially Useful Productive Work) provides them a formal opportunity to explore different areas and have exposure to work experience in electronics, computers, designing, cooking, craftwork, organizing activities in school and in camps etc.

14-25 (Exploratory stage)—This stage is an adolescent stage with a little extension of adolescence through young adulthood. In the middle school one is a teen exploring her/his potentialities and limitations, evaluating them and developing and consolidating definite likes and dislikes for various activities. They are also trying to explore the world of work. At home s/he listens to significant others who serve as role models (parents, elders, siblings, relatives or neighbours), their temperament, potentials and the kind of work they do. The teen is busy trying to understand and relate to their experiences of work, conditions at work, pay scale, relationship and treatment from the boss etc. In the school they are acquiring an understanding of these issues both in informal and formal ways. Informally, the adolescent internalizes the knowledge by observing and interacting with teachers, peers and the environment around them. Among the peer group they talk about their plan for future career and try to understand the merits and demerits of these. Formally, while studying various subjects they acquire a minimum knowledge of different subjects and the relevant applications of it to different occupations. The course contents learnt at school are directly related to certain occupations and indirectly to some others. The different subjects provide to the adolescents an opportunity to explore into the occupations, the kind of work and the personal qualities and abilities required for these. Co-curricular activities also provide opportunities to try out and develop various skills. For example, working for different school clubs, like school magazine, is found helpful in building up interest in journalism. Similarly art, dramatics, cooking, electronics etc. are helpful in understanding and developing interests in these areas and how well he/she would be able to perform. By the time one reaches class IX, one begins to understand to a good extent one's strengths and weaknesses and by class X some crystallization of self-knowledge seems, visible. Certain schools advocate formal administration of Psychological tests by experts for helping students to have their potentials assessed.

The choice of a stream of education at class XI, whether the student will take Humanities, Commerce or Science or a Vocational course, constitutes the first formal challenge in the direction of career planning. This may or may not be a very well thought out decision for many students. In the choice of streams many forces are at work, such as one's ability, interests, exam scores, parental likes and dislikes, peer preferences and choices, teacher suggestions and availability of a subject in a particular school. Often it is seen in practice that more than the interest of the student, emphasis is on marks obtained in class X Board in deciding the subjects or streams in most schools. The society places higher value on Science and Commerce streams, and parents and students too hold these in higher esteem. Thus many adolescents end up choosing subjects that are not in line with their potentials and interests but have higher social value. This gives rise to conflicts and stress, needing guidance for students and adults (parents, and teachers).

It is indeed once they have begun the class XII that most students display a heightened concern about career, as they now directly face the question—what they would do after leaving the school? They start exploring the world of work and seek more career information from school and parents. Some parents try to collect information 2-3 years in advance and frequently talk to the adolescent about various possibilities. Some parents present the information to the adolescent from their perspective, and in a way indicating a choice which they like. Some schools try to organize field trips, visits to some work places and invite guest speakers. Some students acquire vocational maturity and are able to see the relation between their potential and the occupational field they would like to choose. The choice of career may soon narrow down, as many have to begin processing the forms for entry tests for various courses. For some it may be very clear which line they would succeed to go into but for some others it may be a serious issue, particularly for those who do not qualify for their priority choices.

Path to Career Choice

The path to making a career choice for adolescents is not simple and smooth as it is closely intertwined with growing up issues. There is a constant tussle for priority in the resolution of conflicts. The need for developing self-identity and reformulation of self-concept during this period causes struggle between an adolescent and the parent. The adolescent says 'I want to do something different', 'you don't tell me what to do', 'I even want to do what you are telling me to do, but I cannot do it', 'I want to do something that sounds more exciting', 'Please do not force me', 'I want to do what my friends are doing', 'I want to try it out' etc. On the other hand there are adolescents who may be quite unconcerned and living in the present and think it will happen when the time comes. What is actually good for the adolescent leaves a big question mark?

Many parents and teachers sense the difficulties and are concerned about how to help the adolescents in deciding for a career which is so important for them. What line should our ward take, what is best for our ward, we want her/him to be on the top are the concerns for them. Of course, every parent wants the best for their ward, but how to make it happen bothers most of them? In this pursuit at times they often go over board resulting in the experience of high anxiety and confusion. They are confused about thinking what is good for their young ones.

Career Choosing in Different Students

Students encountering the issue of career choices are not all of one type. They can fall broadly in any of the following four or more categories:

1. Good Students Having Clear Choices. The first category includes students who are quite clear about what they want to do after class XII. They have reached a good deal of vocational maturity by now. They are fully aware of their potentials, likes and dislikes and have clearly identified their choice of a particular field. For example, an adolescent is clear that s/he wants to go for chartered accountancy or engineering or medicine or fashion design, while another one may be very sure about wanting to make music as her/his profession. In fact many of these students, after passing class X, have become convinced about a stream they would like to go in, leading into a career of their choice. They enjoy talking about it to different people they come across in order to verify the correctness of their choice. Such students need to be given opportunities to develop their potential in that field. For example, the student aspiring to make a career in music requires pursuing music during senior secondary stage and getting help to go for music coaching rather than over emphasis on academics. They may be given additional exposure, like allowing them to go to concerts. These students already have information about the chosen career, but require more detailed information about different course levels (degree, diploma and certificate) and career advancement in the field, various training institutes and modes of entrance in the training institutes (entrance test requirements, dates, fee structure and preparation etc).

2. Good Students Not Having Clear choice. The second category of students includes those who are good in studies and know that they have to decide about their career, but are not clear about it. They are confused about what can be the best option for them. They do not know really what to do. At best they have some tentative choices. These students need greater clarity about their strengths and weaknesses, interests, achievement to be able to narrow down their occupational choice. They need information on more than one occupation that may be related to their strengths and interests. They need to be informed about the possible courses and related careers so that gradually they can focus on the occupation of their choice. It is possible that some students take little longer than others in making their choice. They may decide to narrow down their choice and yet pursue a general education programme or try out some training course or have job experience in the area of their interest for some time and then finally settle on a career of choice.

A case of unclear career choice had been presented by Tanvi, an all rounder and above average student. She had good general knowledge, was fond of reading, wrote occasionally, enjoyed going for excursions and being with friends. She liked participating in school activities like dance, music, craftwork etc. At home she learnt Bharatnatyam and Kathak. However, she did not excel in any particular subject till she was in class X. In academics her performance often fluctuated between 60-85%.

Her mother worked as a counselor in one school, and she deliberately refrained from putting pressure on Tanvi. Even if her marks fell down, both the parents remained supportive of her. Her friends often wondered how did she escape scolding at home.

By nature Tanvi was a quiet, sensitive and stable child. As she approached class X, she found that other children were already talking about what they wanted to become or which stream they would take up. She also began exploring in her mind what she was good at and what were her interests, but as she did not excel in any particular subject she felt that she had no particular choice. Tanvi turned to her mother for help. In order to help Tanvi make a career choice her mother made her consider her strengths and weaknesses. She was a voracious reader, good at writing and her general awareness was good. She identified various career options related to Tanvi's strengths, such as—Journalism, Mass Communication, Publishing, Study of Languages, Translations, Teaching, and discussed with her. Soon Tanvi arrived at a decision and was able to tell her friends that she would go for Mass Communication.

After class X Tanvi faced the question of the choice of streams. Tanvi was clear about not going into Science stream, but had the conflict of choice between Commerce and Humanities streams. Many of her friends were going for commerce. Tanvi also thought of taking up commerce, but her mother felt that Tanvi would not be able to do well in commerce as her maths was weak. Also for her nature and temperament, commerce may not be the right stream. In order to help her getting convinced really, she advised Tanvi to borrow commerce books from her friend and go through them for 3-4 days. After going through these books Tanvi realized that she would not be able to study commerce for the next two years. Tanvi thus decided to go for Humanities. She felt reassured that her strength was in Social Studies and English and her marks were also higher in these subjects. She took English, Political Science, Sociology, History and Economics as her subjects.

Tanvi performed very well in class XI. Having chosen the subjects of her choice and right potential, she scored above 80% in all subjects. Her confidence rose tremendously and she scored 86% marks in class XII Boards. She managed a distinction in all subjects and 90% in economics. She was among the first five students in her class.

Tanvi got admission to BA (Hons.) in History in one of the topmost colleges of Delhi. While in college, Tanvi did some writing and editing for Wild Life Trust of India, and learnt French. After finishing graduation she had a choice of going for courses in Mass Communications/Journalism/M.A. in History, International Relations, Archaeology, MBA or preparing for IAS exam. She chose Journalism and Mass Communication.

It can be seen that Tanvi proved to be an above average student in the end and managed to perform well with her parents' support and right direction. Parents could have pressurized her in class IX and X or scolded for low marks in maths leading to the habit of telling lies and anxiety, but they did not do so. Rather they encouraged her to focus on her strengths. In class XI, the decision to go for humanities and not commerce was a difficult choice, as commerce was considered to be one up stream. Rather than dissuading the child, parents made her experience the reality by letting her go through the commerce books. The parents displayed confidence in her abilities, which reinforced her self-esteem. Taking subjects of her choice helped her in achieving higher, which in turn enhanced her self-confidence. In college also, she was encouraged to explore various options/areas in which making a career choice would be easier for her. (Appendix II, Careers for Humanities by Kumkum Tondon).

In general, students in this category are unable to decide what to choose because they have not excelled in any particular subject. Such students need help in exploring their interests and flair for a field, even if scoring at par in most. Their other skills such as creative ability, communication skills, outgoing nature and other hobbies should be explored and highlighted rather than putting emphasis on intellectual capability and marks. Writing self-reports can bring out such traits. Opportunity may be given to them to try out and have some practical experience. Extensive information about various fields should be given to them after class XII and graduation.

Kamla was a class X student, who would score between 60-65% in all subjects, and when asked she would not express liking for any particular subject. She was advised to write a page about what she would like to be five years later and then 10 years later. Based on her writings, her teachers and counselor felt that she loved to create new designs and given training may do very well as a designer. She was thus advised to go for Humanities. She got nearly 70% in Class XII Boards and importantly qualified for admission to NIFT.

3. Students Having Unrealistic Choices. Some students have unrealistic career choices. Raghav was a science student. He had been a good student throughout ranking among the top five in the class. In class XI he opted for physics, chemistry, maths and computer science. He started aspiring for entry into an engineering college after class XII. His father being an IIT graduate himself wanted his son to appear for IIT. Raghav was the only child and parents had set all their hopes and aspirations on him. They told Raghav to begin coaching for IIT entrance from class XI itself. There were many other students in the class who were doing the same, but Raghav resisted the idea of joining any coaching in class XI. He was very apprehensive of himself to be able to cope with two things at the same time. He decided to do it after passing class XII. As he was given the feeling that he should always come on the top, there was lot of pressure on him to do well and to hold onto the image of a good student. He asked for extra help in maths and physics, but was not able to do well despite the extra coaching. He even changed his tutors twice. He felt extremely restless before the exams and even after the exams was very unsure of his performance. He scored well in class XII having 91%. His parents pressurized him to appear for IIT exam (AIEEE) with only one month of preparation. Raghav did not agree to appear for the exam as he felt threatened by failure.

After class XII he decided in consultation with his parents that he would drop a year and prepare for the IIT entrance exam. The parents had their mind fixed on IIT and were not able to think beyond. He joined on their initiative one of the best tutorial classes for the preparation of IIT tests. After attending the classes for 3-4 months he felt very unhappy. He became irregular in the classes and started avoiding studies at home. He felt unsettled and ultimately dropped out of the IIT coaching classes. The parents then engaged private tutors to help him cope with studies. He joined another coaching class that taught in smaller groups. Here also after few weeks Raghav felt he could not cope and left. He did not take any test series available for engineering entrance and by January he dropped all the classes.

His inability to adjust and cope with studies caused a lot of anxiety to him and his parents as he had dropped an academic year. He started having feeling of failure and some behavioural problems. He became aggressive and started to get irritated with people at home. He developed some complexes. He would sleep for long hours in the day and would miss meals.

Seeing that Raghav was very confused parents made him join a personality development class and visited a counselor. The help of the counselor and the personality development class made Raghav analyze his own feelings and apprehensions. He found that his main fear was his inability to compete with other students preparing for engineering and to come up to that level. The counselor talked to Raghav about the whole range of courses besides engineering that he could pursue and do well. He managed to shortlist Computer science and Maths Hons, and also took the initiative to explore the possibility of joining some engineering colleges offering direct admission.

The personality development class helped him also in developing other personality attributes, building his self-confidence, overcoming inhibitions in a group, talking to strangers, extending general awareness by reading newspapers etc. He gave up on engineering colleges and started exploring the colleges that were good for Computer Science, as he found he had great liking for it. Finally, he succeeded in securing admission in a reputed Delhi university college in BSc. (Computer Science Hons). This was a realistic choice for him as computer science and maths were his strengths. Now from a feeling of worthlessness and despair, he began to look forward to doing this course and other activities, such as taking up a language class, playing sports and joining a computer club in college.

As this case show, too much of parental emphasis on engineering in IIT was the cause of undue anxiety and stress for Raghav. His strength in maths, and computer science in comparison to physics and chemistry should have been noticed earlier. Consideration should have been given to his self-confidence, shy nature and other personality factors. Undue emphasis on marks from childhood made him over critical of himself, which in turn led to anxiety and lower self-confidence. Choices other than IIT should have been provided to him. A range of courses could have been discussed with him, such as, Computer Science Hons, general Maths Hons or other Maths related courses.

The case of Raghav emphasizes the need of a systematic career planning for adolescents. Too much pressure building at the cost of ignoring the interests and aptitudes of the student adds to confusion, ultimately leading to frustration for the student and parents. Importance should be given to the personality traits. Situation becomes even more difficult when there is wide gap between what the parents want and what the adolescent wants for himself, and what actually her/his capacities are.

At times, the choices adolescents make are distorted or are based on fantasies or are copied from someone they admire. For example a class IX or X student who is just average in studies may say I want to become a doctor. Or a girl of very average looks and height thinks of becoming an air hostess. Or a non-science student desires to be a pilot. Obviously these students lack the information required for entry into these occupations. They are not aware of their own strengths and weaknesses. They have less career maturity. They require information on the requirements of entry to various courses. It may as well be that their choices are made because of the pressure of parents at home, but it does not match with their potential. The parents may also require counseling in some cases.

4. Students Having no Career Plans. A fourth category of students includes those who have not thought of any career plans. They do not have any motivation for a career nor they think it necessary at this stage. When asked they say 'we have not thought about it' or 'first we will finish school studies and then think about it' or 'I will think when the time comes'. They are not conscious that taking up a career needs some planning. They have very little information about the world of work. They are the ones who are not even aware of their own potentials. At the time of choosing the subjects, they chose a subject of their choice or subject related to their past performance, but in no way by seeing a relation to future career. They would like to pursue general education in college. They are happy in their own world. They have very little stimulation in their environment either at home or school. It may be because of the high security provided to them at home and their over dependence on parents. It is seen even more among girls, where it is not considered necessary for them to work and they are expected to be happily confined to home. They never think of work till they finish studies. They may start working with parents, if there is some family business or do whatever comes their way or go by trial and error. Girls may pursue some hobby or do some small jobs and leave after sometime. Home making becomes of prime importance to many of them once they get married and have family. Some may ponder over the question—Is it necessary for every person to make a career if one is happy without it? Or what happens to a person when the circumstances change and one has to work? It may be advisable to motivate even such persons to take some training in a field of their choice that will equip them with some skills to face future challenges positively.

Many students from low socio-economic families drop out of school either because they are not able to meet the set educational requirements or due to the need of working early or the family needing them at home. Their family needs them one way or the other and for them sustenance is important. Many of these adolescents end up working as unskilled workers. It may be better to motivate them to take some training in craft courses and income generating skills that would give them higher income. The socially deprived students, who can not afford to go to institutes located at distances from home, should be informed about the institutes close by. They may also be told about distance learning and vocational training courses. Some parental counseling may be necessary in these cases as they have to understand and recognize the career needs of these students.

It is necessary that the career information given to a student is related to her/his self-perceptions. The individual needs vary and different individuals do perceive different occupations differently. A career that is appealing to one individual may not appear attractive or even acceptable to the other. The occupational information that is congruent with the self-concept of the individual is likely to result in a realistic career choice.

Career Patterns of Different Students

A look into the data on school finishing students demonstrates differences in the chosen career patterns of students in different categories. Some of the career patterns identified on the basis of students' school achievement and the careers opted are discussed below:

High Achievers. Most of the high achievers, even prior to reaching the class XI, have decided to go in a particular stream of studies suitable to their abilities and interests. They are able to narrow down their choice to a particular field of interest e.g. engineering, fashion designing, CA etc. They start preparing for the entry exams along with studies of class XI and XII. They require detailed information about the range of courses and occupations in that particular field. For example, a range of courses for a student having interest in biology may be Medicine, Dentistry, Microbiology, Biogenetics, Pharmacy etc. They also require detailed information about various training institutes in these areas. Too much emphasis on highly esteemed institutes or courses may put undue pressure on some students. There may also be some students, who despite their higher school achievement may not want to go for stereotypical careers, such as medicine for engineering etc. Some of the high achieving students may be non-conformists with high potential to do well in various creative fields. There are examples of some doctors and engineers who became singers or took to civil services. Thus it may be necessary to recognize their other strengths, besides the intellectual performance. Take the case of Ravi. He wanted to go for Engineering, but failed to qualify the entrance exams. His parents took it as normal and it did not make him feel bad. Rather they together with Ravi identified an alternative course. Ravi did a three-year diploma course in Aircraft maintenance which fetched him a high salary job. Some of these students, may become over ambitious and not necessarily more competitive. They have high aspirations, and if they are unable to meet them or are not able to clear the entrance test, they become over anxious. These students require lot of emotional support rather than being subjected to pressure for keeping on trying. They need to be given alternatives to enter the other fields. It has to be accepted by students and parents that not all high ability students have the probability of succeeding to get into the topmost institutes. Some students who pass out of the less known institutes can also do very well in life.

Low Achievers. There are some students who do not score very high in academics. Their performance is always either on the margin or they struggle to reach the next class. Parents and teachers often wonder about their future. In general people tend to look down making them develop a negative self-image. It is essential to help these students in developing some hobbies along with studies. Their parents may be advised to give them opportunities to engage in other creative activities, like, music, painting, theatre, dancing, sports, NCC, public speaking etc. Their strengths should be identified and reinforced through training and recognition. Later, the student can be encouraged to choose a career related to one's potential with the positive feeling of being successful in that area. In classes XI and XII they may be encouraged to opt for vocational subjects rather than academics. They should not be derogated for their not so good academic achievement. Rather their other qualities and interests should be highlighted and developed.

Shivani had delayed development of her milestones in early infancy. She got admission into a well known public school because of her mother, who was a renowned doctor. She pulled through primary school, but at middle school level she had difficulty in coping with academic work as the studies became more demanding. Her problem turned grave as her mother could not devote much time to help in her studies. She engaged tuitions to help her in English, Maths and Science. Somehow, she struggled and found her way through middle school. On reaching class IX the school told parents that she would be promoted to the next class only if she will agree to appear for class X exams through open school and not as a regular candidate. The school was concerned about the school results not getting spoiled.

During this time, Shivani's parents got in touch with a counselor, who suggested to get her enrolled in a less competitive school. Keeping in consideration her family background she was admitted to the public school where other students were also mediocre. She shined among them coming from a good public school background. She was a chirpy girl and had good command on English. Her communication skills were good. Shivani developed her self-confidence as there were few students to compete in the class and she got lot of personal attention. She also picked up in academics and passed class X exam with a good II division. The earlier public school took her back in class XI. As she had shown some interest in drawing, she chose graphic designing, English, Sociology, Home Science and Political Science in class XI. She passed class XII with a good second division.

Instead of going to a regular college she chose to go for a four-year diploma course in fashion designing in South Delhi polytechnic. She did very well in the course as it matched her interests. After completing the course from polytechnic she specialized from NIFT in apparel designing which was a one year course. She then went to America to do a degree course from FIT for two years. Along with the course in polytechnics she joined BA in IGNOU with subjects—English, Marketing, and Export Management. Shivani got job as a designer with a reputed leather bag manufacturing export house and is earning a handsome salary of Rs. 30,000-40,000 per month.

This category students need information on certificate and diploma courses related to their interests, names of institutes (Government & Private) conducting these courses, Polytechnics and ITIs etc. (Appendix II). Along with the Vocational course they can be advised to pursue studies through National Open School or IGNOU (studies through Correspondence) at their own pace.

Students Having Disruption in Studies. The career patterns for students having disruption in studies are different than those of high and low school achievers. These students have not been able to pursue studies in an ongoing and smooth manner due to some special circumstances, such as failure, stagnation, family circumstances, shifting from town to the village, financial reasons, death of head of the family and many more. In certain cases it may become necessary for the person to work. In such cases, the person may be advised to pursue studies either through correspondence or open school system or take a short term course along with the job. There is need to motivate and encourage them to continue studies and advance their training.

Karan lost his father while he was in class XI. His father had a photography shop. As he was the only earning member suddenly the family income became zero. Karan told the teachers that he will have to discontinue his studies to give financial support to the family as he was the eldest child in the family. He said that he will learn photography from a relative for a few months and then start working at the shop. The teachers felt bad for him as he was a very diligent student. They tried to persuade him to somehow manage to continue his studies. They explored with him various means of getting financial help.

Karan approached the school counselor. She gave him lot of encouragement and supported his decision to learn photography. She also told him about the open school (See chapter 6 for details). Karan agreed to do that though with some reservation. By the year end he was running his photography shop and passed class XII from open school. He was very happy. He was encouraged to do further studies from IGNOU.

Students like Karan required assurance, guidance and support when they change from regular school system to a different system and pattern of studies. Parental counseling is also important as their attitudes affect the children. Tips on time management may also be useful for such adolescents. Open school system of studies may lead to carelessness on the part of some students because of too much flexibility in study schedule leading to discontinuation of studies. This needs sustained effort. Information on various short-term training courses, income generating skills and self employment opportunities is also helpful.

Career of Girls. The social contexts in which girls grow and function in India indicate the need of a discussion of careers exclusively for girls. Traditionally, the society considered home making as the prime domain of work for girls. The dominating attitudes of parents and other social pressures inhibited the girls from thinking in the direction of career planning. Girls also showed little motivation and career aspirations, as they were self- diffident. Those who chose a career are mostly in middle level jobs, part time or the jobs which require them to be away from the home for half a day. However, the trend is changing now. More and more girls are opting for higher education and for technical and professional occupations, though their percentage is still lower than boys.

The girls need to be motivated for career planning. This can be done by making them aware of their potentials, providing role models and information about various occupations. They need extra stimulation as the social setting affects adversely their already hesitant attitude towards work. The parents need to be counseled as they influence their career planning and choices. Girls need to be made aware of government policies, facilities and incentives related to girls' education and employment.

Some disruption comes in girls' careers because of marriage and having a family. Some work for a while after marriage and then give up, while some may come back to a job later. Others may continue to work along with a family with some support systems. The rise in the standard of living and the financial needs of the contemporary families require both the husband and wife to work. This will not be possible unless the mind set of the male is changed to help and share the domestic chores.

How to Choose a Career?

The successful choosing of the right career is the desired goal as it can give lot of satisfaction and fulfillment. A career that matches the person's interests and potential would lead to progress and give her/him an identity. This requires knowledge about oneself and knowing about the world of work and then matching of the two. This process has become quite complex now because of the amount of information available from different sources and opinions of persons difficult to ignore. One also has to deal with stiff competition and many types of pressures that threaten to bog her/him down to opt for careers and courses one does not like to do. The choices made by many get thus distorted leading to dissatisfaction and stress.

It is advisable that one should get a good self assessment of one's potentials and strengths, and gain knowledge of various courses and occupations, and then seek a match between the two as much as possible. The chosen career should reflect a combination of attitudes, aptitudes, interests, personality traits and the upcoming opportunities. Those careers should be avoided for which one does not have strong aptitude, as it will not help the individual to rise in career and have satisfaction.

Self-Knowledge. Some persons may use the strategy of knowing oneself as much as possible prior to making the choice of career. How does one perceive one's potentials, strengths and weaknesses, may affect the career choice? A person with limited or inadequate self-knowledge may make an inappropriate choice than a person with adequate self-appraisal. The choice may limit both range and level of occupations. Knowing oneself encompasses knowing one's abilities, interests, aptitudes and values. A number of psychological tests, inventories, check lists and questionnaires are available to assess one's interests, intellectual level, aptitude and adjustment. Psychological testing has to be done by a trained psychologist. However these should not be used in isolation and should be supplemented by other non-testing techniques, such as, observation, self reporting, essay writing, list of pastime activities and hobbies.

The close observations of the parents and teachers and discussing of their opinion with the adolescent may be quite helpful. Adolescent can be initiated to do some serious thinking about one's interests and potentials, hobbies and pastime activities. Preparing a list of their likes and dislikes, strengths and weaknesses, nature and personality (outgoing or shy, communication skills, sensitivity level, aesthetic and creative ability etc.) can help in sizing them up. Writings to describe oneself and self-repots can be other ways. School marks in particular subjects may be used to know the ability in that particular area.

Knowledge of the World of Work. A good knowledge of the range of occupations made available to the adolescent can affect the choice making process. Unless a person knows what all is available, he/she will not be able to have the most suitable option. Adolescent will need to know about the entire range of career options available after class XII. Information about various courses available in Humanities, Science or Commerce should be compiled and given to students. The information given to students should also include: information about inter-related jobs within a field e.g. for science students with biology the choices may extend from medical to courses in para-medical, pharmacy, biogenetics, bio-chemistry, nutrition, dietician, physio-therapist, nursing, laboratory technology etc. Appendix-III). List of opportunities may be made available for career advancement in a particular field. List may also include vocational courses for students stagnating and failing.

Students may be encouraged to access various sources of career information. Published career books are available in the market (Appendix -1). Internet is an upcoming source and provides latest information. Newspaper advertisements and TV provide information about the particular institutes. Schools can give occupational information through posters, charts and bulletin board displays, and organizing career fairs, career talks and field visits. Teachers in the class may try to relate the subject they teach to the different occupations listed. Students may be kept informed of the emerging careers (Appendix III), and referred to various career information centres in city (Appendix I).

Matching the Two. After having a good self-assessment of one's potentials and strengths, and gaining knowledge of various courses and occupations, one should try to match the two as much as possible. The personality traits should also be taken into consideration e.g. outgoing or shy nature, communication skills, sensitivity level, aesthetic and creativity ability etc. For example, a child who likes helping others may be good for social work, nursing or teaching professions, while a child who likes to fiddle with gadgets may be suitable for electronics. A more communicative child will be suitable for social work, sales, PR, while a shy child will be more suitable for a desk job or an occupation which involves more thinking. An aesthetic child may be more inclined towards designing, creative arts etc. Physical attributes also affect the career choice. A child with weak eyesight and weak constitution may not be successful as a pilot or in armed forces, police etc. The chosen career should be a combination of one's attitudes, interests, personality traits and the emotional factors and the upcoming opportunities. Those careers should be avoided for which one has weak aptitudes as it will not lead the individual to rise in his career.

A number of factors are found active in the shaping of the career choices of students:

Age is of primary importance as it brings in vocational maturity in an incremental fashion. As one gets older one tries to accumulate information from multiple sources and sifts through to be able to make a good career choice. Many parents put pressure on their children to opt for a particular profession. One may also be influenced by a person s/he admires or pulled towards a career of peers' choice.

Each person has own nature, aspirations, ambitions, and expectations etc. These also affect the choice of career. Career choices of boys and girls are found to be different. Conventionally boys go for more intellectual, and technical jobs requiring higher physical and mental ability and commitment or in financial jobs, whereas girls choose jobs that require more of human interaction, and involve aesthetic ability etc. The trend has however, changed now. In addition to having access to information, one requires the actual availability of opportunities in the region to allow the making of a good career choice. For example, a person in a hilly region or a village will have access to opportunities in that region only, unless one gets information about adjoining regions and bigger towns.

General Guidelines for Educators/Parents

1. Emphasize Co-curricular Activities and Hobbies. Emphasis should be given to co-curricular activities besides academics, so that students can develop their other potentials and interests besides intellectual pursuits. Parents should help their ward in developing different hobbies from an early age.

School should provide to students opportunities to participate in different activities, clubs and societies. For example, If a student is good in singing, acting, aesthetics or writing ability, it should be recognized and conveyed to them and should be given further training opportunity to reinforce their abilities.

2. Help in Personality Development. Students should be helped in personality development, such as, enhancing their self-confidence, public speaking, organizational abilities etc. Their creative and positive traits may be identified and helped in furthering their strengths.

3. Relating Subject Learning to Work. Different subject teachers should demonstrate how the teaching of their particular subject is related to various careers. This will generate students' interest in that subject and a positive perception of it to do well and explore further opportunities in that field.

4. Help in Career Planning. Students should be helped in career planning, by identifying their interests, aptitudes, strengths and weaknesses. Extensive occupational information should be given through various means and should be told about multiple ways of processing and utilizing the information. Parents may be advised to observe their ward carefully and identify her/his interests and hobbies, before suggesting what one is capable of and what should one try his hands on. It needs to be acknowledged that most persons have a range and combinations of talents that equip them for a number of jobs and not one only.

5. Minimize Pressure. Parents and teachers should not pressurize students for pursuing stereotype careers and/or impose their choices and aspirations on adolescents. This causes conflict for them. They should be encouraged and allowed to go for non-conventional careers if they are interested in those. They should be helped to make realistic and not necessarily the traditional or ideal career choices. Some counseling for parents may also be arranged to have a change in their attitudes towards teens.

6. Give Information to Students:

- Entire range of courses offered at different levels—Degree, Diploma & Certificate.
- Names of Government as well as Private institutes.
- Polytechnics and ITI's.
- Educational and Training facilities in India and abroad.
- Apprenticeship facilities.
- Local and national employment trends and opportunities.
- Occupational structure in the country.
- Income generating skill courses e.g. making soap, candles, envelopes etc.
- Evening and correspondence courses.
- Vocational and short-term courses.
- Financial aid and scholarships for studies (Names of NGO's and Trusts giving financial assistance to students).
- Direct entry jobs e.g. salesman, receptionist, call center etc.
- Business opportunities and loan facilities.

7. Exposure to Career Fairs and Literature. Provide relevant amount of exposure to learn from diverse sources by taking them to lecture, exhibitions etc.

8. Work Exposure. Encourage students to do summer jobs so as to get actual job experience. They should be taken to work places to make them have the feel of the work.

9. Upgrade Own Information and Knowledge. Parents and teachers should upgrade their own information and knowledge about job market, emerging courses and careers to be able to help the students to make better and correct career choices. The globalization of market economies and new developments are speedily changing the job definitions and required skills.

10. Accept Failure as Normal. No one can succeed all the time and in everything. If an adolescent has failed don't belittle her/his self-esteem. Have patience and support the adolescent to try another time with better preparation.

11. Remind Yourself that Choosing a Career is Tough. Making a career choice is not easy. If the adolescent wants to change, help her/him by discussing it with them. Accept a change if necessary.

APPENDIX-I

Vocational Education & Career Information Centers

- **Polytechnics** run by the Board of Technical Education & Private Institutions.
- **Health & Para-medical Institutes** set up by State/Central Government and Private Educational Trusts.
- **ITI Training Centres** run by State Government and Private Education Societies and NGO's.
- **Schools** run under CBSE and State Board of Senior Secondary Education.
- **Distant Learning Education Institutions.**
- **Central and State Open Universities, Central and State Universities.**
- **Engineering Colleges, IIT's and TIT.**
- NCERT—Educational and Vocational Guidance Centre.
- **School Career Corner.**
- **State Educational and Vocational Guidance Bureaus.**
- **Urvi Vikram Charitable Trust, New Delhi.**
- **Usha Albuquerque—Career Information Centre, New Delhi.**
- **Career Launcher.**
- **IQRA Society for Career Guidance, 6-CGO Complex, Lodhi Road, New Delhi.**
- **Employment Exchanges.**

APPENDIX-II

Published Career Literature

- Career Literature Series, State Vocational Guidance Unit, Directorate of Employment, Pusa, Govt. of Delhi.
- Career Directory Series.
- Student Aid Publications (SAP) .
- Caring Career Information & Guidance Series-Vision Publications.
- Directory of Polytechnics in India (SAP Publications).
- The Essential Career Guide to Careers in India—Usha Albuquerque.
- Career Options after 10+2 and Beyond (Humanities & Commerce)—Kumkum Tondon.
- Career Options after 10+2 and Beyond (Science)—Kumkum Tondon.
- Study Abroad by Kumkum Tondon.
- The UBS Career Guide—Jayanti Ghosh.
- Employment News.

APPENDIX -III

List of Emerging Careers

Science

- Information Technology & Software
- Nanotechnology
- Electronics & Communications
- Biotechnology
- Microbiology
- Environmental Studies
- Forensic Science
- Industrial Technology

Design and Arts

- Fashion Design
- Textile Design
- Fashion Journalism & Photography
- Industrial & Product Design
- Furniture Design
- Ceramic Design
- Commercial Art
- Gem & Jewellery Design
- Accessory Design

Aviation and Hospitality

- Air Hostess & Air Steward
- Ground Jobs
- Hospitality
- Tourism

Media

- Graphics
- Animation

- Journalism & Photography
- Advertising
- Script Writing
- TV, Satellite TV

Management

- Rural
- Hospital
- Personnel
- Finance
- Labour Communication
- Call Centres
- Tele Communication
- Public Relations

Others

- Special Educators
- Coaching Centres
- Health & Education
- Event Management

12

Skills and More Skills

Advice is like snow—the softer it falls, the longer it dwells upon, and the deeper it sinks into the mind.

Samuel Taylor Coleridge

Mrs. Chawla the counselor asked Mrs. Verma the class teacher of class X 'how do you feel in dealing with adolescents day in and day out.' Mrs. Verma scratched her head and said it is undoubtedly tough and yet she feels quite overwhelmed by the experience and challenges. Adolescents do have their dreams, adventures, confusions and in general a desire to ride high. They have multiple temptations and excitements around and also, restraints of family, school and society. They indulge in diverse activities some of which are safe but some are wild and risky. Their context is full of opportunities. They constantly battle to balance their needs and preferences with the expectations of parents, teachers and peers. The journey may be less stressful and even pleasant if the parents, teachers, counselors would walk with them and look towards the future for all to come out achievers/winners and happy partners. Parents are not to walk holding adolescent's hand. They need to walk behind to provide support, in the front to show the path, and on sides to keep them on the track. The growing up process makes multiple demands on adolescents. They need to be enabled to acquire diverse skills in areas of cognitive, emotional and behavioural functioning to encounter the challenges. Their training assumes prime importance in a developing and yet tradition bound society in order to help them face the socio-cultural norms, and the effect of exposure to more or less unsolicited technology/media for now and in future.

Needed Skills

As the child makes a passage into adolescence one encounters daily life situations, which make new physical, psychological and behavioural demands. One has to learn how to handle the changes occurring in one's body and thinking. If not prepared these may become traumatic experiences to some. Some develop negative thoughts about self, resulting into various complexes that threaten to hinder the whole process of growing up. The passage from early to middle and secondary school requires students to build up capabilities to deal with the growing academic demands and do well in various curricular and co-curricular activities. They have to learn managing their emotions to be able to put up with periodic excitements and failures in all spheres of life. In addition to the skills to meet the school demands, adolescents have to acquire the skill of maintaining relationships and communication with parents and other members of the family. They have to acquire the social skills of getting along in the peer group to have positive social acceptance and a sense of identity in the group. They have to develop skills to cope with the changes and complexities of the contemporary day-to-day life, such as the change of school, change of residence, separation from parents etc. At each step adolescents face tasks of decision-making and deal with their emotions and feelings.

Different national and international agencies concerned with adolescent empowerment have identified some useful skills that include—self-awareness, empathy, critical thinking, creative thinking, decision making, problem solving, healthy interpersonal relations, effective communication, management of emotions and coping with stress. These skills may be categorized into three broad categories—thinking skills, social skills, and negotiating skills, as one is either doing tasks that require intellectual resources or interacting with people around or negotiating with self or others. The adolescents may be imparted and reinforced these skills through training and practices in family, school and community. These skills are also called life skills, which are defined by WHO as “abilities for adaptive and positive behaviour that enable individuals to deal effectively with the demands and challenges of everyday life”. It is hoped that the acquisition of such skills would enable adolescents to gain knowledge in diverse areas of life and develop such attitudes and skills that would facilitate the adopting of healthy behaviours. In the absence of inner resources, strength and skills to cope with the challenges, adolescents may resort to some inappropriate behaviours, such as running away from the situation (withdrawal, depression or suicides), or to risk taking behaviours (aggressiveness, substance abuse and unprotected sex).

All of these skills are interdependent and inter-related, and are often used in some combination to deal with various situations. Most adolescents acquire these skills to different extent and use them but these need to be reinforced and refined on an ongoing basis. These core skills are briefly discussed here:

- **Self Awareness.** This skill enables the person to have good knowledge of one’s strengths as well as weaknesses of physical attributes, intellectual level, aptitudes, interests, values, personality traits, level of confidence and what one wants in life. Many of the adolescent problems arise due to lack of self- awareness and acceptance, as an adolescent tries to behave like someone else or projects oneself to be a different person. Thus for adequate adjustment in environment it may be necessary to help such an adolescent in learning to make a realistic self evaluation, e.g. ‘I am short’, ‘I am fair complexioned’, ‘I have helpful nature’, ‘I have average intelligence but I am a good orator’ and so on.

The practice of the periodic listing of one’s qualities and traits is found helpful in making one self-aware. The persons may be presented with a list of personality traits to assess themselves such as—happy/sad, friendly/lonely, outgoing/quiet, extrovert/introvert, aggressive/relaxed, confident/shy, formal/informal, helpful, warm, tolerant, aesthetic, creative, intellectual, physically strong/weak, particular, methodical, punctual, emotional, sensitive, charming, hard working etc. It is expected that a self-aware adolescent would conduct oneself better than a non self-aware one. All adolescents should be encouraged to develop positive personality traits. They should be given opportunities to explore their potential and to try out certain behaviours.

• **Empathy.** Feelings are the essence of living. For basic healthy living along with being self-aware it is important to understand others too. Often adolescents centre around their own concerns and feelings. To develop and sustain friendships and relationships they need to know and be sensitive to other peoples' feelings and situations. This will help them in better adjustment in their environment.

Adolescents can be taught to empathize with others. To develop sensitivity in them, they can be made to feel how others feel in a particular situation. They can be given certain situations and asked for responses. For example—'Meena was crying, what could have happened to her?' 'Simi was upset as she lost her fancy pencil box. How she may be feeling?' Late teens may be asked—'Shanker broke his friendship with his friend, how he must be feeling?' 'Ridhi is very quiet today, something wrong must have happened with her'.

• **Critical Thinking.** Adolescents should be made to face the day to day situations on their own and do their own thinking rather than waiting to be handed down the ready made solutions to every problem. They should be helped to learn how to comprehend a situation, analyze the situation and weigh the pros and cons of it, and identify different alternatives/solutions. It is important for them to learn to identify and understand the factors that may be influencing the situation. For example, in a given situation one should be able to think 'What can this situation do for me? What choices do I have. What can be the outcome of each choice I make? In what way the choice 1 will be less desirable than the choices 2 and 3 and so on?' When Rishi faced the situation in the exam paper to leave a question, in case of not knowing the full answer or construct a logical answer from partial information, Rishi found the second choice better than first, as it helped him score 50% more marks on it and thus raised his total score.

• **Creative Thinking.** It implies thinking of more than one possible ways and solutions or find a somewhat unique solution to deal with the same situation. It is looking beyond the usual way of imagining, conceptualizing, doing and evaluating the things, in a way out of the box thinking. For example, 'when a student has to bring something for the project work to the school and gets very upset when it is not available, s/he should be encouraged to think of the possible alternatives that may be available rather than going through the pain of being stuck at one thing and continue to be upset.' Or 'if an adolescent has not succeeded in getting the career of her/his choice, one should be encouraged to think of other alternative careers rather than feeling depressed or resorting to a negative behaviour'. This habit will help adolescents cope up better with ups and downs of daily life situations with out getting disturbed.

• **Problem Solving.** Adolescents tend to face almost on a daily basis, a number of problematic situations that need resolutions. Conflicts arise when an adolescent feels helpless as nothing can be done in the given situation and feels short of resources to cope up. One has to solve these conflicts and dilemmas by assigning some priority to the problems. For example—one has to attend the problems of coming to a class knowing that teacher is going to punish, having to prepare for a test next day while the friends want to make a programme to go out to whom adolescent can not refuse, or organizing an exhibition in school or a party at home in a short time.

Parents and teachers need to train them from the childhood itself in skills of problem solving. They can pose certain problem situations to them and make them think of the solutions and decide on their own. For example, parents may ask them that 'if one day you happen to miss the school bus what will you do?' 'If mummy is not home one day to help you, whose help will you take to prepare for the test?' Parents can assign them the small tasks. As they grow up more freedom and opportunities to find solutions to their own issues may be given. Adolescents will learn to think of the possible solutions, making use of available resources and ruling out whatever is not possible. Parents and teachers should let them explore more possibilities and find solutions rather than being rigid with their own point of view.

- **Decision-Making.** As the society has become more complex with so many pressures, temptations and influences on adolescents, it brings in situations where they need to make their appropriate choices. For example 'they may be tempted to bunk a class to watch a game', or 'they may want to go for a movie but parents are not giving permission', or 'they have to resolve issues like pressure from close friends to take alcohol but it clashes with their personal values'. Adolescents are required to make the decisions which are in congruence with their own level of satisfaction and the socially acceptable norms. They should be able to say 'no' to the risky and undesirable temptations at their own initiative and not succumb to pressures. Parents may set boundaries and good value system from the beginning.

Adolescents should be trained in systematic problem solving. Some of the steps involved in solving the problems and reaching a decision may be specified as:

- Identify the issue.
- Think of various ways or alternatives to solve it.
- Weigh the consequences of each alternative i.e. how these options will affect you and the people connected with you now or in future. What past experiences are influencing the choices e.g. any negative or positive experience.
- How the choices relate to the goal?
- Look at the positive aspects of different solutions and then choose the best alternative.
- Implement the decision.

Adolescents should be enabled to take decisions while being encouraged to consult parents, teachers and others to feel reassured.

- **Effective Communication and Relationship Building.** Communication forms the bases of all relationships. It may be verbal or non-verbal. Adolescents encounter various situations at home, at school, and in society that require them to interact with persons around them, parents or other family members, peer group, teachers, or people in community. They do need to learn the art of living together, care and share with each other, and maintain harmony and peace in the community. When they acquired the skill of developing healthy relationships and can communicate effectively their feelings to others, they would also meet many of the important adolescent needs (affiliation, achievement, power, recognition etc.).

An effective communication between teachers and pupils would facilitate the learning process and make pupil participation in many of the activities in school pleasant. Good communication with peers would give feelings of trust, social acceptance and sense of belongingness in the group, and facilitate the development of positive self-esteem and personal identity. At home adolescents need to maintain healthy interactions with parents to share their feelings and emotions and to get reassurance of their love and support. For example: 'the adolescent may ask the father—If it is O.K. to say 'no' to a relative/friend without being seen as rude' or 'can she reciprocate if a male classmate compliments her and wants to be friendly and vice versa' or 'can s/he choose acting as a career instead of going for academic subjects'. Open communication would give them the opportunity to seek the needed information and advice on sensitive issues related to friendships, sexual health, academics, careers and other growing up processes.

Adults need to attach importance to the non-verbal cues, as adolescents often find it hard to verbalize the sensitive issues. For example, if 'your adolescent seeks your consent by saying can I stay over at....' Show acceptance so that adolescent can talk about the underlying needs. In the absence of adequate communication with parents and teachers adolescents turn to hide their feelings, look for help outside the family to wrong sources or resort to some risk taking behaviour. As a matter of practice, all adolescents should be allowed to identify one adult of their choice whom they can trust to talk and seek advice.

Effective communication requires correct usage of language, good listening skills, patience, conveying understanding to what the other person is saying and being non-judgemental. Adolescents should be encouraged and given adequate opportunities from early years to express themselves freely. For example: 'if the adolescent is narrating a party experience to you, do not interrupt and shun her/him.' Lack of understanding on the part of adults, their dominating attitude and repeated criticism forms a barrier to communication. On the contrary, the adult practice of letting them speak in the presence of others can help in developing trust and enhancing the self-confidence of adolescents.

In schools teachers talking to students in general, taking interest in their background and talking to the students individually encourages good relationship between pupil and teachers. A teacher having good rapport with the pupil can be very supportive and can prevent the pupil from exposure to risk behaviours.

Adolescents should be encouraged to extend their relationships to relatives, neighbours and friends. Developing good relationships builds support systems for adolescents. For adolescents it is easy to share their feelings and opinions in their own age group, thus making friends should be encouraged. They can share their ups and downs with them and get their support and reassurance to fall back on them in times of need. They have common interests and their' spending time together can help in strengthening their friendship further. They should be taught to appreciate others qualities and achievements and not be critical. They should develop the habit of paying compliments to others. Trust, caring, empathizing with others and reliability are the components that help to sustain friendships. Parents and teachers should be proactive in inculcating and reinforcing these qualities in adolescents.

• **Coping with Emotions.** Emotions are inherent to living beings. Feelings of joy, sadness, love, hate, jealousy, anger, all are part of life. Expressions like 'I am so angry', 'I feel frustrated', 'I feel cheated', 'I feel jealous,' 'I feel bored', 'I feel excited' are commonly made by adolescents, which they want others to understand. The adolescents thus need to learn how to deal with emotions.

To make them familiar with their own feelings and emotions they should be made to identify and write simple things as—'what things make me happy?' or 'what makes me feel sad?' or 'what makes me angry?' Adolescents should be helped to become familiar with their emotions and the underlying feelings they may have related to these. 'When they are happy what do they feel—excited, pleased, good etc, and what behaviour they display—Do they start jumping/Do they smile/dance/sing. Similarly when they are angry, what they feel—Do they get irritated/Do they feel frustrated/Do they feel betrayed or hurt etc.? and what behaviour they display—Do they start shouting/Do they kick/ Do they fight/Do they act aggressive?.'

The intense emotions may have negative effects on normal functioning. One may say 'I am off mood I will not do this or I want to remain In my room whole day.' Adolescents may be helped to develop the skill of managing their negative emotions in healthy ways. First step would be to recognize own feelings that I am so angry or hurt or irritated or sad, unhappy and then sharing and communicating one's feelings with friends or others. In case of intense negative emotions having a glass of water, leaving the situation temporarily and doing some physical activity is helpful. Writing the feelings on a paper and discarding it gives relief. Grownups showing that they understand their emotions and feelings and empathize gives them relief. Similar support they can get from their peer group.

• **Coping with Stress.** A fundamental cause of stress in teenagers may be the passage from childhood itself. There are significant body changes taking place making it hard to accept and manage one's body (the handling of puberty, dressing). The issue of identity comes to the fore making the adolescents wonder about their position in comparison to others. There are pushes and pulls arising from peers and parental expectations.

There is high degree of competitiveness in school, jealousy among peers, lack of understanding by parents, teachers and peers, and there are situations of being disregarded/belittled and/or not given due rewards/fair treatment, which many adolescents may find difficult to cope with.

The causes of stress may be internal and/or external, with one or more acting simultaneously on the person. The internal causes are developmental and part of the growing up process e.g. shyness, lack of confidence, sensitivity etc. These become stressful in the absence of information to manage oneself and need psychological support. The external causes are inherent in the expectations and pressures put by the parents, teachers or society at large. Parents and teachers may set very high standards that do not match with adolescents' capacities. The ensuing stress may be related to the choice of a career line or difficult social relationships (Parental expectation of son getting into IIT is too much for the son).

Certain stresses are situational and/or may be even transitory. It needs to be stated however, that some amount of stress is helpful to productivity, as it leads to being active and doing hard work, such as studying hard or self-improvement. The stress beyond one's tolerance level becomes harmful and a cause of concern. For example, too high a pressure on students for studying and achieving perfect/not accepting failure are stressful situations leading to the choice of unwanted and risky behaviours. The undue emphasis on girls to look beautiful makes one tense and non-productive. The resulting behaviour may be the difficulty in doing even the routine work. The adolescent may feel confused and lose focus.

One's reaction to stress may be physical or emotional. Some adolescents may stay very relaxed in the event of getting marginally acceptable (60%) marks, where as some others find it very stressful. There are certain others who get very stressed even on getting 90% marks. It all depends on personal expectancy levels. Adolescents will not feel stressed if realistic expectations are put on them in terms of their behaviours, achievements, relationships. They need emotional support when stressed out. Encouragement and reinforcement may be given to the shy and lesser confident ones. A warm and supportive atmosphere will encourage communication and sharing of their concerns with the parents or the trusted ones. Systematic problem solving skills should be developed in adolescents. They should be helped to acquire the skills to overcome shyness, avoid misunderstanding, initiate and carry out conversations, and effectively handle social situations.

However, it may require the use of certain stress management technique if an adolescent is stressed out. Deep breathing, yoga, meditation and other relaxation exercises are helpful. It is essential to remove the adolescent from the stress causing situation. Adolescent, may be helped to brainstorm various possible solutions to the problem and in developing skills. Clapping and laughter therapy also relaxes a person. Change of activities, playing a short game even during examination, listening to music is recommended for the stressed outs.

Adolescents can manage stress if they have acquired the skill of handling failure to some extent. They should internalize that the success and failure are part of life and two sides of the same coin. One has the opportunity to succeed and fail in diverse situations, such as examinations, competitions, and building relationships etc. They need to accept that even failures present opportunity to grow, if they stay positive and act with conviction. For example 'one may say I am O.K. I will work harder and succeed.' Their self-image and self-confidence need to remain positive to be able to live with some stress and look at challenges in a positive light.

Summary Guide for Parents

No.	Issues	Parenting Guide
1.	Developing Assets & Challenges	• Prepare yourself & the adolescent. • Adolescence is a period of rapid physical, emotional, cognitive and social changes. • Different domains of development are inter-related. • Teens' concern for identity is normal. • Accept challenge to your authority. • Teens are most vulnerable group. • Adolescents need information & guidance.
2.	Body Image	• Do not ridicule teens. • De-emphasize colour. • Appreciate one's natural looks. • Help to accept natural growing up changes. • Help not to sway with things media glamourizes. • Help to develop hobbies. • Appreciate their personality characteristics & talents. • Discuss qualities of chosen icons other than physical attributes.

3. Eating Habits	• Have frequent talks on food, health & nutrition. • Create awareness of anemia. • Inculcate proper food attitudes from beginning. • Involve children in weekly menu planning. • Add essential nutrients. • Make combinations to enhance food value. • Be informed on new food recipes. • Make proper time allocation to food. • Emphasize regular physical exercise & breakfast. • Control junk food. • De-emphasize figure consciousness.
4. Sexuality in Adolescence	• Inform Teen on what, how & why of sexuality & sex. • Give information on pubertal changes. • Monitor use of media & protect against unwanted exposure to sexual images etc. • Teach values related to sex & sexuality. • Maintain continuous support & communication. • Encourage hobbies. • Take sexual feelings as natural & deal maturely. • Recognize sexual exploitation & sexual abuses. • Give information about contraceptives, pregnancy, STD and HIV.

5. Identity in Adolescence	• Help develop positive self-image. • Allow freedom to explore. • Make home a safe base. • Evolve consensus on basic values & rules. • Have good listening skills. • Set clear ground rules. • Specify sanctions in advance. • Manage disagreements. • Avoid corporal (physical) punishment. • Set example. • Trust each other to contain peer influence. • Allow privacy. • Accept & support identity efforts.
6. School Achievement	• Set a study schedule & follow it. • Advocate regular practice. • Help them use appropriate learning method. • Make learning enjoyable, diversify teaching. • Make them do homework regularly. • Allot a noise free study place. • Some competition necessary. • Identify & work on reasons for fall in performance. • Accept individual differences in children. • Avoid over scheduling & over load. • Set realistic expectations.

7. Net Technology	• Encourage positive use of internet. • Teach effective search & exit strategies. • Develop sense of right & wrong in use. • Block certain sites for early adolescents. • Place computers in shared areas. • Sensitize for misuse/unwanted exposure to net & media. • Tell precautions to be taken on net social networking sites/SMS. • Inform of new security checks. • Imbibe safe & ethical practices in teens. • Encourage judicious use of time on media
8. Adolescent Communication	• Be patient. • Do not over react. • Be a good listener. • Accept adolescent needs. • Add humour & laughter as natural. • Over-strictness & nagging cause barriers. • Show empathy. • Encourage making friends. • Encourage trusting, complimenting & helpfulness. • Use good language in communication. • Give responsibility. • Teach dignity of labour.

9. Behavioural Issues	• Take early note of cues. • Understand pressures operating on adolescent. • Help adolescent to express her/himself. • Recognize individual uniqueness. • Help in redefining personal goals. • Identify one's strengths, alternatives/opportunities. • Discourage severe punishment. • Insist on adherence to rules. • Show acceptance & create sense of belonging. • Encourage good moral values. • Set example. • Be positive in approach • Seek professional help if needed.
10. Smoking & Drugs	• Act early to make them stop. • Keep communication open. • Teach them to say 'no'. • Encourage sharing of feelings & support seeking. • Help accept failure & distress. • Help find alternative sources of fun. • Be role models. • Have no drugs around. • Recognize multiple consequences of drugs. • Emphasize personal growth. • Help develop personal & social skills. • Improve your parenting skills. • Encourage rule compliance.

11. Career Guidance	• Upgrade own information & knowledge. • Understand needs of your ward & career. • Help find own strengths & weaknesses. • Relate subjects taught to various careers. • Give information of all levels (degree, diploma & certificate). • Expose to career fairs & literature. • Encourage work experience & summer jobs. • Encourage realistic choices. • Do not over emphasize a particular career/course. • Inform about related careers in a field.
12. Skills & More Skills	• Help understand ones strengths & weaknesses. • Learn to understand others feelings. • Think of more than one solution & ways of solving problems. • Help weigh pros and cons of action. • Learn problem solving & decision making. • Help developing effective communication skills & healthy relationships. • Help coping with emotions. • Help to develop stress management skills & strategies.

Index